Stuffed grape vine leaves (page 28).

Bean soup (page 34).

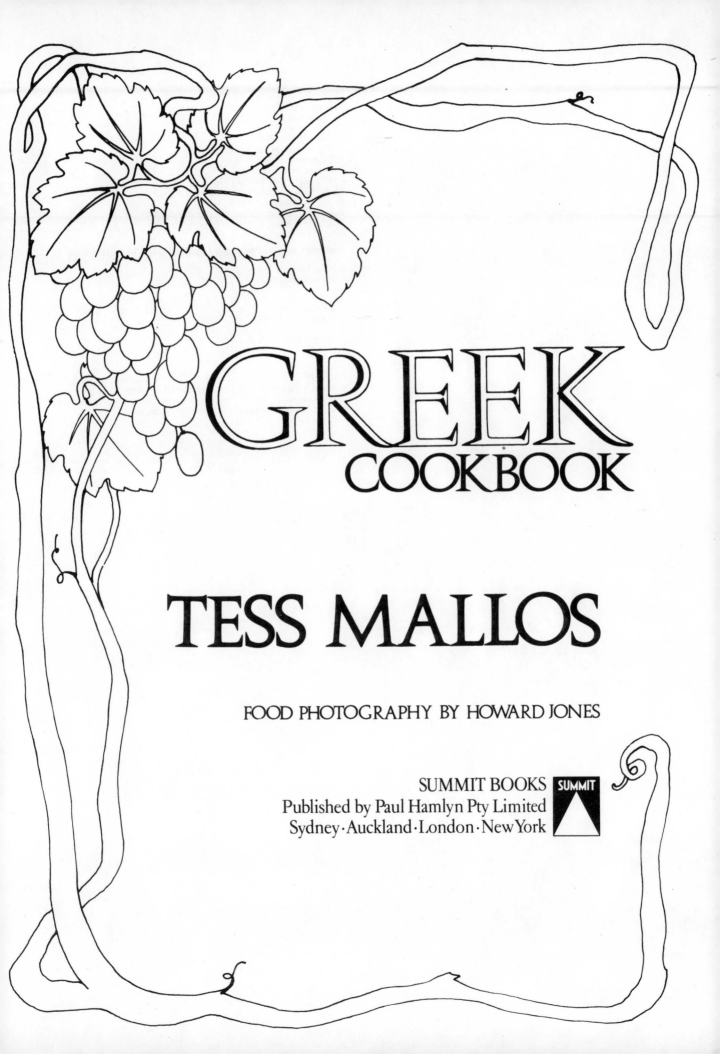

GREEK
COOKBOOK

TESS MALLOS

FOOD PHOTOGRAPHY BY HOWARD JONES

SUMMIT BOOKS
Published by Paul Hamlyn Pty Limited
Sydney·Auckland·London·New York

Published by Summit Books
176 South Creek Road, Dee Why West, NSW, Australia 2099
First published 1976
2nd Impression 1976
3rd Impression 1977
4th Impression 1977
First published in this format 1978
2nd Impression 1979
3rd Impression 1980
© Copyright Tess Mallos 1976
Produced in Australia by the Publisher
Typeset in Australia by G.T. Setters
Printed by Toppan Printing Co. (Singapore) (Pte) Limited
38 Liu Fang Road, Jurong, Singapore 22

National Library of Australia Cataloguing-in-Publication Data

Mallos, Tess
    Greek cookbook.

    Index
    Bibliography
    ISBN 0 7271 0287 7.

    1. Cookery, Greek. I. Title.

641.59495

CONTENTS

GUIDE TO WEIGHTS & MEASURES

The metric weights and metric fluid measures used throughout this book refer to those of **The Standards Association of Australia** (AS 1325 1972). A good set of scales, a graduated Australian Standard measuring cup and a set of Australian Standard measuring spoons will be most helpful. These are available at leading hardware and kitchenware stores.

- The Australian Standard measuring cup has a capacity of 250 millilitres (250 ml).
- The Australian Standard tablespoon has a capacity of 20 millilitres (20 ml).
- The Australian Standard teaspoon has a capacity of 5 millilitres (5 ml).

All spoon measurements are level spoonfuls.

Note: For successful cooking use either metric weights and measures **or** imperial weights and measures — do **not** use a mixture of the two.

WEIGHT, VOLUME AND LIQUID MEASURES

In all recipes, imperial equivalents of metric measures are shown in parentheses, e.g. 500 g (1 lb) young beef. Although the metric yield of cup or weighed measures is approximately 10% greater, the proportions remain the same.

The following tables are extracted from conversion equivalents adopted by the Cookery Sector Committee of the Metric Conversion Board, (Australia).

IMPERIAL			METRIC	
Liquid Measures	Cup Measures	is replaced by	Cup Measures	Liquid Measures
1 fl oz				30 ml
2 fl oz	¼ cup	..	¼ cup	
	⅓ cup	..	⅓ cup	
3 fl oz		..		100 ml
4 fl oz (¼ pint US)	½ cup	..	½ cup	
5 fl oz (¼ pint imp.)		..		150 ml
	⅔ cup	..	⅔ cup	
6 fl oz	¾ cup	..	¾ cup	
8 fl oz (½ pint US)	1 cup	..	1 cup	250 ml
10 fl oz (½ pint imp.)	1¼ cups	..	1¼ cups	
12 fl oz	1½ cups	..	1½ cups	
14 fl oz	1¾ cups	..	1¾ cups	
16 fl oz (1 pint US)	2 cups	..	2 cups	500 ml
20 fl oz (1 pint imp.)	2½ cups	..	2½ cups	

Mass (Weight)		Mass (Weight)
½ oz	is replaced by	15 grams (g)
1 oz	··	30 g
2 oz	··	60 g
3 oz	··	90 g
4 oz (¼ lb)	··	125 g
6 oz	··	185 g
8 oz (½ lb)	··	250 g
12 oz (¾ lb)	··	375 g
16 oz (1 lb)	··	500 g (0.5 kg)
24 oz (1½ lb)	··	750 g
32 oz (2 lb)	··	1000 g (1 kg)
3 lb	··	1500 g (1.5 kg)
4 lb	··	2000 g (2 kg)

IMPORTANT POINTS

New Zealand, Canadian and **American** weights and measures are the same except that the Australian Standard measuring tablespoon has a capacity of 20 millilitres (20 ml) whereas the New Zealand, Canadian and American Standard measuring tablespoons have a capacity of 15 millilitres (15 ml). Therefore, all tablespoon measures should be taken generously in New Zealand, Canada and America.

Although accurate measuring is not crucial for many recipes, it is important that standard measures be used for baked goods. The baked goods recipes in this book have been tested with both the 250 ml cup and the 8 fl. oz cup. When using the latter, the only area where the ingredients do not decrease proportionately is in the eggs used. However, it is only necessary to reduce the egg sizes. Use 60 g (2 oz) eggs with the 250 ml cup; use 55 g (1¾ oz) eggs with the 8 fl. oz cup.

It is also important to note that the imperial pint (Australia and New Zealand) has a capacity of 20 fl. oz, whereas the Canadian and American pint has a capacity of 16 fl. oz.

OVEN TEMPERATURE GUIDE

Description of oven	Celsius °C	Fahrenheit °F
Cool	100	200
Very slow	120	250
Slow	150	300
Moderately slow	160	325
Moderate	180	350
Moderately hot	200	400
Hot	220	425
Very hot	230	450

The above temperatures relate in general to electric ovens. Decrease by 10°C or 25°F for gas ovens or refer to the manufacturer's temperature guide. For temperatures below 160°C (325°F) do not decrease the given temperature.

ACKNOWLEDGEMENTS

For some time I have wanted to share with you the pleasures of Greece and the Greek cuisine. This I have tried to accomplish by combining information from many sources — eating Greek food, cooking Greek food, talking Greek food; photographs, recipe books, travel and history books; and inevitably and happily, a tour of Greece which enabled me to see and explore the Greek culinary tradition.

The results are contained in these pages, but they would not have been achieved without the assistance of many organisations and individuals. In particular I want to express my sincere gratitude to Qantas Airways Limited for the opportunity to visit Greece for research and location photography; to Howard Jones for his excellent food photographs; to my husband, John, for his constant encouragement and location photography; to Rod Burchett whose skilful artwork brought together locations and relevant foods; and to my editor, Peter Hutton, whose enthusiasm for Greek cooking made my task so much easier.

As often as possible I have used Greek pottery, cooking utensils, handcrafts and textiles in the illustrations. The embroidery seen in the illustrations on pages 88 and 89 is the exquisite work of Miss Xeni Giannaki, formerly from the island of Cephalonia and now residing in Sydney. To Xeni, my warmest thanks.

In Greece I was indebted to the following organisations and people for their co-operation and assistance: The National Tourist Organization of Greece; Aristotle Anagnostou of Athens for the photographs used on pages 21 and 117; Mr Panapoulos at Potteries of Greece, Amarousion, Athens; Blue Sea Line, Athens; Epirotiki Line, Piraeus; Hellascars, Athens.

In Australia I was generously assisted and advised by Professor Alexander Cambitoglou of the Department of Archaeology, University of Sydney; E. Calligeros and Sons, Wine Merchants, of Sydney; Mr. N. Stavrou of Mediterranean Wines Pty Ltd, Sydney; A. & P. Antoniou Pty Ltd, Wine Merchants, of Sydney; Mrs. June Hazell of the Bay Tree, Woollahra.

I must also offer a grateful and sincere thank you to my relatives and friends who helped in so many ways.

Tess Mallos

A COOK'S EYE VIEW OF GREECE

The cuisine of the Greeks has been profoundly influenced by more than 3,000 years of history, by the nature of the climate, the land itself and the surrounding seas, and by invaders and other visitors — though their food has always been, and remains, essentially and irrevocably Greek. Their zest for living, their love of music and dancing and talking (there's a touch of Zorba in every Greek), are all reflected in their hearty approach to good eating. Thus food, traditions, history and the lifestyle of modern Greece are inextricably mingled — and thus, too, one must approach the cuisine of Greece in the same way as the Greeks do in order to appreciate it fully.

This introduction is therefore something of a kitchen-chair travelogue: a brief guide to the regional culinary delights of Greece, a nostalgic back-tracking for those of you who have been there, a glimpse of toothsome enjoyments awaiting those who plan to visit Hellas.

A balmy summer evening is perhaps the best time to capture the feeling of Greece and its foods. After the quiet of siesta you will see the townships come to life as families stroll along the plazas and quaysides. They might take refreshment at a taverna, dine at a restaurant, sip coffee at a *kafenion* or indulge in a piece of delicious, honey-sweet *baklava* at a *zaharoplastion* (patisserie) without a thought for calories — and during the course of the evening they may well stop at all of these places.

The tavernas are the most frequented of the establishments catering for the inner man. Here you can sip an *ouzo* or quaff a cold beer while enjoying one or more of the offered *mezethakia* (appetisers) — a Greek does not drink alcohol without having something to eat, even if it is only a nibble.

As a visitor you may have problems in choosing the right restaurant in some places. Be guided by the fact that the best are usually those most favoured by the locals. Once inside, ask if you may see what is offering in the kitchen instead of consulting the menu. This is an accepted procedure in most restaurants, with the chef happily and proudly showing off the results of the day's labours and sometimes recommending a particular dish. The meal is served with crusty bread, wine or beer and the inevitable carafe of iced water. Fruit in season is offered for dessert, but if coffee is ordered it will come to you from a nearby *kafenion* since one establishment will not encroach on the special preserve of another. The coffee will arrive on an ingenious tray designed to keep the heat in and the dust out.

If fruit is not quite enough for afters, find your way to the nearest *zaharoplastion* if you're prepared to ignore the threat to your waistline! In addition to making typically Greek pastries, cookies and confections redolent with honey, spices, many kinds of nuts and fruits the *zaharoplastis* creates tortes and pastries of French origin with flair and expertise.

You will soon discover that Greek cooking, with its bold flavours and ample servings, is not *haute cuisine* — and who wants that all the time, anyway? But it does have an appealing character of its own. The Greeks make the most of the humblest of foods; their culinary innovations are unique and at times quite surprising — *kolokitho-korfathes*, for example, are rather like *dolmathakia* (page 28) but use the flower of the squash instead of vine leaves as the wrapping. The emphasis is always on the freshness of the ingredients, although Greek cooks are experts at preserving nature's bounty for later use — not the conventional vegetables and fruits that the Anglo-Saxon races preserve so well, but vegetables such as eggplant pickled in vinegar (page 101); crocks of tomato paste put down with olive oil acting as a seal against spoilage (page 101); and the peel of citrus fruits preserved in a thick syrup (page 100).

The next dozen pages will take you on a hedge-hopping, criss-crossing, 3,000 kilometre tour of Greece as a *mezethaki* before the recipes that follow — from the islands of Thera and Kythera in the south to mountainous Macedonia in the north; eastward from Corfu in the Ionian Sea through Skopelos and south-east to Cos; and finally, after a time-capsule trip spanning thousands of years, to Athens.

But to begin at the beginning, we must start with Crete and the legendary kingdom of Minos. *Bon voyage et bon appetit* — or, as they say in Greece, **Kalo taxithi ke kali orexi!**

CRETE

The pit of coals glows warmly, now and then spluttering with little bursts of flame as fat drips from the pig roasting on the spit above. Freshly caught fish sizzle in a pan of olive oil. The fisherman's son brings a basket laden with crabs, setting them down near the bubbling cauldron. A medley of aromas fills the air as the bread is set aside to cool.

Out over the stubbled fields of just-reaped grain the vines are dripping grape with the promise of a good wine to come. A boy is searching through the fig tree looking for a late-ripening fig, sweet memory of earlier fruit spurring him in his search. Nearby his father is shaking the almond tree, a sheet spread out on the ground to catch the falling nuts. Soon he will have to harvest the olives, for last year's oil is nearly finished.

Crete today? No! It is a scene of the Crete of yesterday — three and a half thousand years of yesterdays — and yet it could well be Crete now.

The civilisation which flourished in Crete until 1400 BC is called the Minoan. Sir Arthur Evans, the archaeologist who spent the autumn and winter of his life excavating and reconstructing the site of the palace of Knossos, named the Cretan civilisation after the legendary priest-king Minos, known through Greek mythology.

The Egyptians of that period called these ancient inhabitants of Crete the Keftiu, but what they called themselves remains a mystery for their earliest form of writing (Linear Script A, as Evans called it) has not yet been deciphered, and many facts about this first civilisation of the Western world are still unknown. Perhaps they will never be known. But archaeological finds show that the civilisation was of a high standard unknown elsewhere in the Western world at that time. These finds draw a fairly accurate picture of the Minoans' foods and the way they could have been prepared.

Giant storage jars at the site of Knossos were used for oil and wine, and olive and wine presses confirm that the Minoans and other inhabitants of the island knew how to utilise the olive and the grape. In fact the seafaring Minoans carried on a thriving export trade in wine and oil, a trade confirmed by the finding of Minoan oil and wine jars in lands bordering the Mediterranean as far west as Spain.

Beef, mutton and pork featured prominently in the Minoan diet. The horned sheep and short-horned cattle which graze on Crete today are similar to those which served the Minoans and their predecessors. Meat was spit-roasted or boiled in giant bronze cauldrons now on display at the museum at Heraklion. No bones of birds were found, but a three-legged clay platter with six holes could have been used to hold eggs, and perhaps to cook them. Fish was certainly a part of the Minoans' diet — bones found in a cooking pot show that fish was probably boiled, but bronze frying pans found indicate that it could also have been fried. The shells of lobster, crab and edible varieties of shellfish suggest that the sea was a major source of food; octopus and squid may have been included for they often appeared in pottery decoration.

The grains used were barley and wheat. No ovens have been found, so bread was probably cooked on hot stones and would have been unleavened.

Other Minoan foods were leeks, beans, chick peas, lentils, vetches, almonds, dates (from warmer southern Crete), figs, pomegranates and honey. All in all, the Minoans had a balanced diet. They used milk and this could have been made into a cheese or used as curds — a pottery vessel with perforations looks so much like a curd strainer that it is difficult to imagine any other use for it.

The Minoans were not Greek, but their influence on, and association with, the Mycenaean Greeks on the mainland has been confirmed in archaeological finds which positively link these two great civilisations. The Minoan influence on early Greek cooking would be difficult to dispute.

THE SPORADES
SKOPELOS

It is a long jump from Crete to the Sporades, and particularly the Northern Sporades, but historically the link is there.

Mycenae fell to Dorian invaders from the north in about 1100 BC, and the next four hundred years were Greece's Dark Age. During this period many of the displaced Mycenaeans migrated east and north-east to establish new settlements on islands (now part of the long Sporades group) in the Aegean and on a narrow strip of Asia Minor (modern Turkey). The area was called Ionia — not to be confused with the Ionian Islands and Ionian Sea on the western side of Greece.

Life centred on the sea. The Ionians sailed it — and colonised other Mediterranean areas as far west as Spain and north to the Black Sea. They fished it — and gave birth to one of the classics of cooking.

The fishermen of Ionia would spend days at sea, and for sustenance they looked to their catch. One piece of equipment, which always accompanied them, was the *kakavi*, a three-legged pot. To cook their meal they would set a fire in the boat or on a deserted beach. Into the *kakavi*, filled with crystal clear water from the Aegean, would go all the smaller fish of their catch, olive oil, onions and saffron from Asia Minor (saffron is rarely used in Greek cooking today, but was greatly favoured by the ancients). To this flavoursome stock, when cooked, were added slices of larger fish, lobster and prawns. A few minutes more of cooking, and the *kakavia* was ready.

When the Ionians colonised Massilia (today's Marseilles) in the sixth century BC, this fish soup was enthusiastically adopted by the Massilians. They called it *bouillabaisse* after the *bouillotte* (pot) in which they cooked it, just as *kakavia* was named after the *kakavi*.

The Northern Sporades today — Skopelos: Life is still bound up with the sea and the fishermen on Skopelos still prepare *kakavia*, although now this is usually done in the home. Saffron no longer spices it (tomatoes are used for colour and flavour) and only occasionally, if ever, is there lobster to add to home-cooked *kakavia* — although there are plenty of lobsters offered at restaurants catering for the tourist trade in this popular region. A modern recipe for *kakavia* is given on page 33, and is a refined version of the Skopelos dish.

Another Skopelos speciality is *kolokitho-korfathes* (literally 'squash flowers') — a mouthful of a name for a dish which is a very pleasant mouthful indeed! The recipe is the creation of the Vlahakis family.

As every home gardener knows, not all the flowers of the squash vine bear fruit; some just bloom and die. But on Skopelos the flowers are picked before the sun's rays close them, and are then filled with a mixture of onion fried in olive oil, grated zucchini, rice, herbs and seasoning. Each flower is carefully rolled up like a *dolmathaki* and placed in the pot. They are then finished in a similar fashion to *dolmathakia* (page 28) and left to cool in the pot before being served as an appetiser.

If you have no squash vine, but plan to visit Skopelos, call in and see Nikos Vlahakis at the Siren Restaurant and try them there.

THE DODECANESE

COS

During the Golden Age of Greece food, to the inhabitants of Cos, was more than a means to appease hunger. They were conscious of the relationship between food and their health. Their diet was well balanced: meat, fish, eggs, cereals, milk, cheese, fruit and vegetables. They were aware that their bodies required more food in winter than in summer; that meats and fish boiled or baked were better for them than fried foods. Even the obese were made conscious of the fact that they would probably not live as long as those of more slender build. Exercise was an important part of their daily routine for its importance in relation to good health had been clearly recognised.

This enlightened society owed its chance for better health to one man, a physician named Hippocrates. Taught by his father, Heracleides, one of a long line of priest-physicians, Hippocrates did not believe that the gods were responsible for man's ills. Through his observations, his meticulous recording of case histories and his reasoning, he took medicine away from the mysticism and superstition with which it had been shrouded for hundreds of years. He made medicine a science.

His aphorisms and other writings contain many other instructions on regimen for the young, the aged, the invalid and for man generally. Many of his statements are as applicable today as they were more than two thousand years ago.

Growing bodies need the most food; soft, moist foods should be given in infancy and during feverish illnesses for they are more easily digested; people in good health should not take purgatives; how often food is taken, and in what quantity, depends on age, work, habit, season and locale; food and exercise work together to produce good health since eating alone does not keep man well.

As well as making observations on the life expectancy of the obese, Hippocrates gave advice on how to lose weight. He recommended that exercise should be undertaken on an empty stomach. While still panting and hot from exertion one should drink some diluted wine (not very cold). The meal should follow and consist of meat well seasoned with sesame, sweet spices and similar additives. It was recommended that the food be rich so that the appetite would be satisfied with very little of it. Only one meal a day was to be taken; there were to be no baths; one should sleep on a hard bed; and walk as much as possible clad in light clothing.

Hippocrates' advice to thin people who wished to put on weight was to do the opposite of what he recommended for obese people; in particular they should not exert themselves on an empty stomach.

Roots, seeds or leaves from more than 400 plants were used by Hippocrates in his remedies. Herbs were so generally recommended that home cooks took to adding quantities of the more aromatic herbs to foods in order to promote good health.

His most popular medications were *ptisan*, a concoction of barley and water, either thick, strained, cold or hot according to the reason for its administration; *hydromel*, a mixture of honey and water; and *oxymel*, a mixture of honey and vinegar. These were also used in conjunction with other remedies.

For a patient suffering from empyema, the following was prescribed:
Cut bulbs of squill, boil in water and drain. Add fresh water and boil until bulbs are soft. Triturate (grind) finely and mix in roasted cumin, white sesame seeds and young almonds pounded in honey. Form into an electuary and administer, followed by sweet wine.

The remedy for dropsy does not sound quite as pleasant:
Take three cantharides (a type of beetle), *remove their heads, feet and wings.*

Triturate their bodies in three cyathi of water and when the person who has drunk the draught complains of pain, apply hot fomentations. The patient should be first anointed with oil, should take the draught on an empty stomach and eat hot bread with oil afterwards.

Other beverages administered in treatments were made from raisins, grape skins, wheat, saffron, myrtles, pomegranates, apples, medlars, dates and asses' milk. Hippocrates did not think very highly of administering water to patients. He usually prescribed it in very small quantities or with a dash of wine added to it.

Coriander was recommended for heartburn and, if taken before retiring, it promoted sleep. Marjoram was used to treat haemorrhoids. Garlic, although believed to cause flatulence, indigestion and nausea on occasion, was considered a good diuretic and recommended for those who planned to drink to excess or who were already intoxicated. Although Hippocrates conceded cheese to be a very good food for those with whom it agreed, he did not regard it favourably since he claimed it caused flatulence and constipation because of the rennet or fig juice used to make the curd. To a long list of foods Hippocrates attributed certain qualities, and related these to their action on the body. His directives were the result of his almost lifelong observation of the effect of various foods on body function.

Cos today: The Coans are as proud of Hippocrates as were their ancestors who benefited directly from his skills. Herbal remedies are still administered to the sick. Chamomile and sage teas, often with the addition of lemon juice, are the most widely used, not only in Cos but throughout Greece. Practising herbalists are still as prevalent in Greece as they are elsewhere.

THE CYCLADES

THERA

Recent discoveries on this volcanic island in the Cyclades show that it was once part of the Minoan empire. The eruption of its volcano about 1400 BC caused the cataclysmic disaster which ended the Minoan civilisation. Today in Thera (it was named Santorini by the Italians, but recently it has reverted to its ancient name), archaeologists are uncovering a city dating from the Minoan era — and there is convincing evidence that it is the legendary Atlantis.

But even before this discovery, there had been other finds in the vicinity that threw light on the eating habits of the ancients. Cheese strainers and the remains of cheese confirm that the Minoans included this in their diet. Oyster, murex and limpet shells point to their use as foods. The discovery of fish hooks confirms at least one of their methods of catching fish. Food was probably spiced because the remains of coriander and anise were among the discoveries. Snail shells were found in one dwelling in a situation that indicated their use as a food — snails are still a popular food in Greece.

Thera today: Although the climate is hot and dry for a good part of the year, Thera's volcanic soil produces a variety of crops. The island rises straight out of the sea, and evidence of its volcanic nature surrounds it. The plateau bears barley, grapes, peas *(fava)*, pistachios and tomatoes.

Thera's tomatoes are small but very sweet and firm, and they make excellent tomato paste. The island had a thriving cottage industry in tomato paste until other islands began to grow tomatoes on a commercial scale and factories took over the process. Today the inhabitants make it for their use alone, although tomatoes are still sent elsewhere.

The plateau is dotted with large, whitewashed concrete pits. Here grapes are crushed, the juice running through a hole into vats. After fermentation and settling, a crushed white rock called *aspropetro* is added to the wine for fining; this was one of the ingredients used in ancient times for the same clearing process.

After the crushing the pits are washed out and whitewashed again. The lime kills any micro-organisms, but by the time of the next crushing no lime remains. The pits are scrubbed well before the grapes are put in and trampled.

This is one of the wine pressing methods used in Greece in areas where yields are comparatively small. Home pressings are done with a small press usually made of copper.

Thera produces barely enough wine for its own use, so the only chance you would have of trying their quite excellent wines is to visit the island. Ask for Santoriniotiko, a white wine; Nychteri, a semi-dry red; and Vino Santo, a sweet dessert wine.

Thera is famous for its *fava* or yellow split peas. The volcanic soil is apparently responsible for the flavour that distinguishes Thera's *fava* from those produced elsewhere. Split pea purée (page 31) is a favourite dish in Greece, particularly during times of fasting.

NAXOS

The largest island in the Cyclades, Naxos is very fertile and famous for its potatoes. Many of its seed potatoes are exported to Europe and to other areas of Greece. Ironically, Naxos' seed has to be imported because its own, while growing well elsewhere, does not do so well locally.

There is an interesting story about the adoption of the potato as a food in Greece. In the early part of the nineteenth century an enterprising merchant brought a cargo of potatoes from the New World. He moored at the wharf in Piraeus and tried in vain to sell his load — the locals would have nothing to do with this strange vegetable. After a couple of unsuccessful days, the crew reported to the merchant that some potatoes were missing. What should be done about it? The merchant, an astute businessman, told them not to be concerned. The pilfering continued for the next two nights, after which the merchant issued instructions that the cargo be heavily guarded. He then set up a stall and sold out almost immediately. The locals had found, after their clandestine activities, that this was a very fine vegetable indeed!

Naxos also produces very fine stone fruit and is famous for its citron. This lemon-like fruit is used to make a speciality of the island — citron liqueur. Two varieties are made: one is very sweet, and bright green in colour; the other is clear and rather dry. The *zaharoplastia* stock liqueurs if ever you wish to try it.

MYKONOS

One of the most popular of all the Greek islands, Mykonos at times exudes a cosmopolitan air yet still retains its essentially Greek character.

At night the quayside is a surging mass of humanity; every restaurant, taverna and *kafenion* is packed — and will stay that way till late at night, for the Greeks dine late in the evening and dinner may not begin until 10 or 11 o'clock (although many appetisers will have been sampled in the bars, *kafenia* and *zaharoplastia*).

All day the spits have turned, first cooking the chickens, pork and lamb for the midday meal, then replenishing the kitchens for the evening onslaught. The range of dishes offered is extensive and the fish dishes, using locally caught fish, are particularly worth trying.

On a rise behind the quayside town you will see four impressive windmills, but only one is decked with sails and still functional. The owner knows it is not financially rewarding to keep the mill operating, but he does so out of respect for tradition — and the tourists.

Think 'bread', and you'll probably think 'cheese'; think 'bread' in Mykonos, and the cheese will be *kopanisti tiri,* a speciality of the island. Made from a mixture of goat's, cow's and ewe's milk, curded, strained and kneaded, then matured in clay pots for 12 months, this cheese is sharp, has a peppery flavour and is delicious spread on fresh, crusty bread. Many tavernas will supply it on demand.

SYROS

To the Greeks, Syros is the traditional home of *loukoumia,* known elsewhere as 'Turkish Delight'.

As the inhabitants of Syros tell the story the Turks, during their occupation of most of Greece between 1453 and 1829, took a liking to this delightful confection and carried the recipe back to Constantinople, thenceforth claiming it as their own creation. (This is just one of many examples of the controversy about what is originally Greek and what is originally Turkish in Greek cuisine.)

The firm of N. Stamatelaki and Son is one of the largest producers of *loukoumia* in Syros, having begun business in 1837 as the first commercial manufacturer. Today the firm's products are much sought after in Greece, and are exported to the United Kingdom and Germany. Available flavours include rose, *mastica* (reminiscent of aniseed), orange, lemon, citron, coconut, walnut and almond. A good *loukoumi* is light and tender, and those of Syros are just that — the Turkish version, according to Mr Kourkoumari (grandson of the founder, and the present owner of the firm), is elastic in texture and therefore inferior.

One requirement for a good *loukoumi* is the right water. Syros is blessed in this regard. Water, sugar and cornflour are cooked in a copper vessel, and a powered mixer stirs the gelatinous mixture constantly for two hours as it boils. Flavouring, colouring or nuts are added and the paste is then spread on a floured wooden frame. Powdered sugar is sprinkled on top and the paste is left for 24 hours to set. It is then cut and tossed in powdered sugar for its traditional coating.

KYTHERA

Legend tells of Aphrodite rising from the sea and going immediately to Kythera — which is proud to be known as the Island of Aphrodite. Even though the worship of gods and goddesses belongs to an era long since past, the Greek is a romantic at heart and would not deny any association with the glorious world of Ancient Greece.

Because of lifelong habit and a desire for self-sufficiency, Kythera's inhabitants still prefer to make their own wine and cheese, preserve their fruit in various ways and make good use of the abundance nature provides.

These skills and practices do not of course belong to the Kytherians alone (you will find them throughout the islands and in rural areas on the mainland), but because they are typically Greek the foods and culinary styles of Kythera demand a close look.

Cheese: The most popular cheese made in the home is *mizithra* (page 105), a mild cottage cheese. Although the Kytherians make the curd with rennet from the stomachs of slaughtered kids, the favoured method is one from ancient times in which the milky sap of the fig tree is used. The sap is used in various ways. One interesting method utilises a fresh twig which is well washed and bruised with a mallet. Goat's milk is brought to the boil and one part of water is added to three parts of milk to break down the strength of the rich milk and to cool it. The milk is then stirred in a rotary motion with the bruised twig. As the fig sap acts on the milk, the liquid begins to change direction of its own accord and there is no more stirring as the curd is made. The curd is poured into a wicker strainer and left for a day to drain. The *mizithra* is then ready to be spread on bread or *paximathia* (dry toast); with fresh fruit and a glass of wine, who could want more!

Mizithra is also dried to a hard cheese of strong but good flavour and used as a grating cheese for pasta dishes. It must be drained for twice as long as the softer cheese, and is then turned out of the strainer, coated well with salt and left for many days in a cool place until dry and hard.

Figs: The figs of Kythera are plump, juicy and as sweet as honey. Some of the first green figs are picked when no bigger than the first joint of a man's thumb. These are made into a spoon sweet, usually stuffed with a blanched almond (page 98).

From ancient times figs have been preserved by drying. They not only add variety to the diet, but are eaten for the medicinal properties which are attributed to them.

The figs are picked when fully ripe and placed stem up on a loosely packed bed of straw. After drying for two or three days in the hot sun (they are covered each night with sheets), each is turned upside down and pressed gently to flatten it without splitting. After a few more days of sun the figs are put into a slow oven for half an hour to dry them completely. They are then strung on strands of dried grass called *vroulo* and hung in the storeroom.

Another favoured method involves cutting through to the base of the fig in four segments, leaving the sections joined at the stem. Each fig is spread out flat and dried in the sun. When it is dry enough, but still slightly sticky on the fleshy side, chopped almonds are pressed on, a second fig is placed on top and the two are pressed together. These are also dried in the oven, and are a delightful confection.

Grapes: Enough has been written about winemaking without going into detail about the methods used in Kythera. It is sufficient to say that a clan picnic can be an inebriating experience since it is mandatory that everyone's wine should be sampled! Grapes that are not used for wine, or for immediate eating enjoyment, are dried in the sun for later use. Currants are used in cooking, and raisins (*stafithes*) are eaten as a pleasant snack, usually with almonds from the almond trees.

Olives: Several varieties of olives are grown, some for the table, some for the olive press. Each household does its own pressing.

To harvest the olives, sheets are spread out under the trees and the branches beaten well to rid them of their fruit. They are then sorted according to ripeness, the green olives being preserved separately from the softer black olives since it takes longer to rid them of their bitterness. The olives are layered in wicker baskets with salt, and the top covered with a cloth. They are then left in the sun until all the bitter juices run out. During this process they are tossed occasionally. When the olives lose their bitterness they are ready to store in wooden casks. Although wrinkled in appearance, they soon regain their plumpness when placed in vinegar or olive oil. (See page 98 for further details on preserving olives.)

Nature's gifts: Although herbs grow profusely, few of them are dried for later use. Parsley, rosemary, mint, dill, fennel and thyme are preferred fresh, and many of them are available for most of the year because the winter is mild. However, sage and *rigani* are gathered in large quantities for drying. The sage is only used to brew sage tea. If you ask for tea in rural areas in Greece, sage tea is almost always served; with a good squeeze of lemon juice, and sweetened with honey, it is most refreshing.

Rigani (wild marjoram) and parsley are the two most popular culinary herbs. *Rigani* flavours lamb, fish and ground meat dishes. Although oregano is a substitute for *rigani*, it does not have quite the same pleasant though pungent flavour.

Chamomile (*Anthemis nobilis*) carpets the spring countryside with its tiny, daisy-like flowers. Each family gathers sufficient for its needs, dries the blooms and stores them for brewing chamomile tea. It is widely used throughout Greece as a remedy for stomach upsets and colds, and as a tonic.

Clumps of golden broom seem to be wherever you look in the spring. The stems, after a lengthy process of beating, soaking in running water and combing, yield a fibre which is woven into cloths on home looms; these cloths are used mainly as ground sheets during the harvesting of olives.

The fields also provide various greens for the table. Dandelion leaves (*rathikia*), a type of mustard green called *vlita* and wild asparagus are boiled and served with olive oil and lemon juice. The *rathikia* and *vlita* are rather like endive and chicory in flavour and are best gathered before they flower.

Globe artichokes grow wild in the fields, among rocks and on the roadside. Though smaller than those cultivated commercially elsewhere, they are more flavourful and are cooked in many ways (see pages 74-6).

With fish freshly caught, lamb or kid from the flocks, fruit in abundance and a vegetable garden that extends the length and breadth of Kythera, the inhabitants are fortunate indeed.

THE PELOPONNESE

The time: around 600 BC; the place: Tegea, south-east Arcadia, in the Peloponnese; the event: Atalanta is to race Melanion; to the victor: Melanion's head if Atalanta wins, Atalanta's hand in marriage if Melanion is the victor; the outcome: Melanion wins with the help of three golden apples from the Garden of the Hesperides given to him by Aphrodite.

What fruit were these golden apples? They could well have been a new, exotic fruit introduced to the area which took the fancy of the story tellers of the time. Opinions vary, and there is never likely to be a definitive answer, but it seems likely that the golden apples were citrons, quinces or pomegranates, all of which were known to or celebrated by the classical authors of Ancient Greece.

Fruit abounds in the Peloponnese today. All varieties of citrus, cherries, apricots, apples, peaches, quinces and nectarines thrive throughout the province.

Citrus groves along the Gulf of Corinth flank each side of the old road from Corinth to Egion. It is a fragrant journey when the trees are in bloom and a colourful one when the fruit are ripe. Even the black asphalt road looks more attractive with its roadside piles of bright-hued fruit awaiting carriers for their journey to the tables of Athens.

Of all the fruits it is the lemon which is most used in Greek cookery. The prince of Greek sauces, *saltsa avgolemono* (page 36) and the delicate *avgolemono soupa* (page 32) are two wholly Greek recipes which, although simple in concept, must rank high in world cuisine.

Lemon juice flavours lamb, young beef and pork, whether grilled, roasted or used in the Greek version of a fricassee. Poultry benefits from the use of lemon, which is used not only to whiten the flesh but also for the delightful flavour it adds. It is unthinkable to serve any grilled or fried seafoods without lemon or a dressing containing lashings of it. Cooked green vegetables must be dressed with lemon juice and olive oil; once tried, it will become as firm a habit as it is with the Greeks. Globe artichokes, asparagus, Brussels sprouts and broccoli, *youvarlakia* (page 50) and *dolmathes* (page 59), finished with *saltsa avgolemono*, are all superb.

Of the lemon nothing is wasted. Its peel is made into a sweet preserve called a spoon sweet (page 100) or glacéd by the *zaharoplastis*; its grated rind flavours cakes and sweet breads; its blossom is used for a spoon sweet made similarly to rose petal jam (page 100) but only the petals should be used; its leaves are boiled and the water used as a rinse for the hair, leaving it shining bright and subtly perfumed. Medicinally the lemon is used to flavour herbal teas such as sage and chamomile and the Greeks also regard it as a remedy for colds and influenza.

Vineyards around Patra, the province's capital, Rion, Achaia and Nemea produce a fine range of wines which are exported widely. See pages 108-9 for those wines readily available outside of Greece.

Kalamata, in the southern Peloponnese, is renowned for its olives. Though not large, they are considered the best flavoured olives of all Greece, and are exported world-wide.

The olives of Tripolis are worthy of mention if only for their size. One ripe, preserved olive weighs about 15 grams (half an ounce) — and they are very flavourful. Another speciality of Tripolis is the pickled sprigs of the caper plant. The capers themselves are pickled but, to make the most of the caper plant which grows wild throughout Greece, the locals also pick young, tender sprigs. These are boiled three times in fresh changes of water, then in salt water. They are drained well, placed in jars and covered with hot vinegar. They are ready for use after one month. Some restaurants in Patra serve the olives and pickled caper sprigs of Tripolis.

CENTRAL GREECE

Messolonghi lies at the head of a large saltwater lagoon which is a favourite spawning ground for the grey mullet. Unfortunately for the mullet their roe is considered a great delicacy by the Greeks. The fish are trapped in cane weirs and deftly speared by the fishermen. The roe, if intact when removed, is salted, dried in the sun until very firm, then coated with beeswax to preserve it further. It is a deep amber colour when dried. Called *avgotaraho* in Greek, it is known elsewhere, particularly in England, as botargo. Peeled of the wax and skin, and thinly sliced, it is eaten with crusty bread as a most flavoursome appetiser, although it does tend to stick to the teeth. *Avgotaraho* is available in season at Greek fishmongers and food stores in other countries.

Any damaged roe is skinned, preserved with salt and is used to make the famous *taramosalata* (page 30). *Tarama* is also mixed with mashed potatoes and other flavourings to make a type of rissole.

From Itea on the Gulf of Corinth, olive trees (around five million of them) begin their seemingly endless spread across the plains at the foot of Mount Parnassos. Amphissa, the main town in the area, exports the black, juicy olives and olive oil. Olive harvest time in November is a time of much dancing, feasting and merriment since the area's olives are vital to the economy.

Easter in Arahova is a memorable experience. On Easter Sunday morning this mountain village gradually becomes shrouded with a pall of smoke as the Easter lambs are cooked, either in private courtyards or communal pits. During the week following Easter Sunday the villagers dress in their traditional costumes and perform their folk dances in the square.

Levadia, on the Athens side of Mount Parnassos, is a popular stop with those travelling to Delphi because the town specialises in *souvlakia* (page 46).

MOUNT PILION REGION
Makrinitsa looks down from its lofty perch to Volos, the main town in the area and a port of departure to the Northern Sporades.

Fried salt cod (page 42) and garlic sauce.

Skewered lamb on a *foy foy* or charcoal brazier (page 46).

You can only enter this picturesque village on foot or by donkey. The air is crisp and cool on a hot summer's day, sharpening appetites. The taverna in the town's square, shaded by plane trees, offers the usual dishes — and a speciality of Makrinitsa called *spetsiofayi*. Its main ingredient is a locally made pork sausage, sliced and fried with eggplant, capsicums and tomatoes.

The Pilion area bears fruit and nut trees in abundance. Some of the walnuts are gathered when green and made into a spoon sweet. Entire walnuts (the thick outer covering with the immature nut inside) are boiled until tender. The thin, dark outer skins are removed and the walnuts are finished in a sugar syrup.

Tsangarada is in the midst of a forest of chestnut trees. In season, vendors sell roasted chestnuts in the streets of the town.

Chestnuts are used not only as a snack but also in meat cooking (often replacing potatoes), and they are essential in stuffings for turkey and goose.

Across from the Pilion region lies Skiathos, one of the islands of the Northern Sporades. Pine nuts come from the groves of the stone or umbrella pines growing on the island. These seeds are much used in Greek cooking.

THE IONIAN ISLANDS

CORFU

Although Corfu has its own regional dishes, it is for lobster *(astakos)* that the island is renowned.

The Corfu lobster is actually the spiny lobster *(langouste* in French) and not the crayfish or crawfish *(écrevisse)* which is a freshwater crustacean; spiny lobsters are often mistakenly called crayfish. A characteristic of the Corfu lobster is its deep crimson colour which changes to bright orange-red when cooked.

At Paleokastritsa, a picturesque bay on the west coast of Corfu, each restaurant has its own lobster cage in the crystal clear water of the bay. When the lunchtime orders for lobster are complete, a boy wades out to the cage to bring in the number required. These are then cooked and served to order. They are boiled in water with mustard and vinegar added, and served either hot or cold with oil and lemon dressing, or cold with freshly made mayonnaise and a sprinkling of capers. They are also grilled in their shells and served with oil and lemon dressing (see page 43). Freshly caught lobster, eaten within sight and sound of the sea, is a gastronomical experience always to be remembered.

Glyfatha, a long sandy beach on the west coast, has restaurants at the northern end of the beach. They also serve lobster but orders must be placed very early because the cages are not within wading distance of the shore as they are at Paleokastritsa.

The regional dishes of Corfu are *sofrito* (page 56), *bourtheto* and *pastitsatha*.

Sofrito is a tangy, garlic flavoured braise of *moshari*, which is yearling beef. The Greeks always translate *moshari* as 'veal', but it is not the milk-fed veal known elsewhere.

Bourtheto is a fish stew flavoured with onions, olive oil, tomatoes, paprika and cayenne pepper. The last two ingredients are not very Greek at all, but probably were introduced by one of Corfu's many past overlords.

Moshari is also used in *pastitsatha,* a stew served with pasta. It is very similar to *kapama* (page 62).

Numbulo, a very tasty sausage with a bacon flavour, is well worth trying if you ever visit Corfu. The island is also famous for *fraules,* tiny aromatic and very sweet strawberries.

The island has many vineyards, olive groves and citrus orchards. The rural areas are exciting to visit at harvest time.

If you drive off the beaten track (it is very easy to do) you would seem to go back one hundred years or so. Peasant women, carrying their burdens on their heads, their faces almost covered with scarves and their bodies clothed in long home-spun gowns, will shyly make way for you to pass in your hired VW or motor bike. Yet these same women, on festive occasions, are resplendent in the provincial dress — richly coloured, heavily embroidered, bedecked with golden coins and jewellery, and their hair entwined with multi-coloured ribbons.

Corfu is a pot-pourri of Venetian, French, Italian and English influences, for all of these people have been its masters. But it still remains essentially, vitally Greek.

NORTHERN GREECE

Macedonia stretches across Northern Greece from Epirus in the west to Thrace in the east. The cold mountain streams and lakes of this ruggedly beautiful region are hosts to a variety of freshwater fish, trout being the most prevalent.

Trout fishing is one of the attractions of Metsovon, a picturesque mountain village in north-eastern Epirus on the road linking Eastern and Western Greece. Equally attractive is the colourful local costume that is still worn by many Metsovon villagers, particularly the womenfolk. It is not uncommon to see them decked out in their finery as they draw water from the well or carry trays of cookies to the *fourno* or bakery. Metsovon seems to have been ignored by time, and few visitors would want this to change — although you might wonder whether the presence of tourists has encouraged the inhabitants to retain their individuality.

Some of Greece's best hunting areas are in Macedonia and Thrace. Quail, turtle-dove, partridge, wild goose, duck, woodcock, hare and wild boar, when their hunting is permitted, add variety to the menu of those fortunate enough to bag them. The recipe for *laghos stifatho* (page 54) can be used for game birds.

The two major cities of the area, Thessaloniki and Alexandropolis, have excellent seafoods. Black caviar is a speciality of Alexandropolis. Both cities have many waterside seafood restaurants, and the prawns, mussels, oysters, lobster and various fish of this northern region are said to be the best in Greece.

THE SARONIC ISLANDS

If you find that your stay in Greece must be brief, but would like to visit a Greek island or two, the ferry trip to Hydra is ideal.

Only a little more than three hours from Piraeus, with brief stops at Aegina and Poros, the trip is almost enough to satisfy a visitor — almost, because the Greek islands cast a spell, and you will not be satisfied until you have visited and enjoyed many more than one.

AEGINA

Your first stop on the way to Hydra is Aegina. If you intend staying longer at this island, take an organised day cruise to Aegina and Hydra for the ferry to Hydra stops for only a few minutes at Aegina.

The island played a prominent role in the history of Ancient Greece. Inhabited in the late Neolithic period, it was influenced by Minoan Crete and conquered by the Dorian Greeks in 1000 BC. Aegina struck the first Greek coinage about 650 BC with its badge, a sea turtle, on one side of the coins. Of great importance commercially for several centuries, Aegina eventually sank into oblivion after falling out with the Athenians about 400 BC.

When the ferry stops at Aegina have a few modern Greek coins on hand to buy some of the pistachio confectionery for which the island is famous. At the turn of the century wealthy Athenians built summer villas on Aegina and planted pistachio trees around them. Today the locals have groves of pistachio trees throughout the island. The nuts are delicious as they are — but even more delicious when made into pistachio nougat, coated with toffee or pressed thickly over *pasteli,* a honey and sesame seed wafer.

The island also has deposits of a white clay which is shaped into traditional pottery. It is the only area in Greece where such clay is found and the pottery is worth seeking out for it chills the water or wine stored in it.

HYDRA

Two hours after leaving Aegina, the ferry reaches Hydra. Its beauty lies in the picturesque port. The hills show the heat of the summer sun, but in spring the island is truly beautiful, particularly when the almond trees are in bloom.

Hydra is famous for its *amigthalota* (page 92), a cooky (or perhaps more a confection) made entirely of ground almonds, sweetened slightly, flavoured subtly and bound together with egg white. The paste is shaped like little pears with a clove inserted for the stem, and after a slow baking it is dipped in powdered sugar. The *zaharoplastia* in Hydra always have a good stock on hand.

On Hydra there are many grand houses, more than 200 years old, which once belonged to wealthy sea merchants. It was through their contributions that the Greeks were able to begin their efforts to cast off the Turkish yoke.

The largest of these houses belongs to the Athens School of Fine Arts where artists from all over the world (some of recognised merit, some of promise on scholarships) may stay for a short while to work. Very few of the other houses are open to the public, and of those most are owned by the Government.

ATHENS

Like all cities, Athens attracts much of its population from far beyond its own boundaries. The shepherd comes in from the hills; the sponge diver from Kalimnos; villagers from the remote mountain areas of Northern Greece and the equally remote islands in the Southern Aegean. And one talent common to all is their culinary skill.

Thus the food of Athens is the epitome of all that makes up the Greek cuisine. At first sight this may not be apparent, but gradually you will begin to appreciate the variety of Greek cooking. The home kitchen shows even more variety, and it is a pity that restaurants do not make greater use of popular home recipes.

THE TAVERNAS

By far the most popular place for refreshment, liquid or otherwise, is the taverna. In summer the tables and chairs spill out across the pavement, promenade, plaza or seashore in the city and suburbs of Athens. All manner of refreshments are served, and *mezethakia* (appetisers) are the speciality. Because of their desire to please tourists, many tavernas in the heart of Athens include non-Greek foods in their menus; but if the taverna has a predominantly Greek clientele the variety of local food is limited only by the availability of ingredients and the ingenuity of the cook.

Plump green and black olives, cubes of *feta* (often bathed in olive oil), anchovies in an oil and vinegar dressing, crisp young radishes, wedges of young cucumber and sun-ripened tomatoes — these are the simpler *mezethakia.*

Salads served as appetisers are quite different from one's usual idea of a salad — sometimes they are a puréed mixture, sometimes a more identifiable mixture of cooked or raw vegetables with a tangy dressing or the powerful but delicious *skorthalia* (garlic sauce). *Taramosalata*, a purée of smoked cod or mullet roe, and *melitzanosalata*, an eggplant purée (page 30) must rank high among the world's dishes for flavour and excellence, though they are a far cry from a conventional salad.

Seafoods served include pickled octopus (page 27), which is quite delicious, but more appealing when stripped of its rather off-putting suckers — it has a flavour similar to lobster; prawns baked in a tomato-wine sauce with *feta* cheese melting on top; delicious fried *kalamari* (squid) served with garlic sauce or lemon wedges; crisp-fried *marides* (smelts); fried mussels.

Hot *mezethakia* include crisp, flaky cheese and spinach triangles or rolls (page 29), delectable morsels encased in *filo* pastry as thin as tissue-paper. Or try hot *dolmathakia* (vine leaf rolls, page 28) stuffed with a meat and rice filling and served with egg and lemon sauce. But just as good are cold *dolmathakia* with a rice filling, sometimes spiked with pine nuts and currants, sometimes with tomato and herbs; cooked in olive oil and lemon juice, *dolmathakia* need no other accompaniment, except a chilled white *retsina*, the pine resin flavoured wine for which Greece is renowned. *Keftethakia*, small fried meat balls fragrant with herbs (page 50), and *feta*, *kefalotiri* or *kasseri* cheese squares are fried quickly in butter and served with a generous squeeze of lemon juice. Small squares of *moussaka* and *pastitso* are also served hot.

The list of *mezethakia* is endless. Almost always accompanied by chunks of crusty bread, a variety of them makes a good meal. Since the Athenian dines late, *mezethakia* serve to quieten the pangs of hunger until dinner, which could be taken near midnight.

THE RESTAURANTS

Restaurant menus are rather standard. *Moussaka* (page 52) is to be found on most of them, as are *papoutsakia* ('Little Shoes', page 53) which are halves of eggplant or zucchini filled with a meat stuffing. Then there are *souzoukakia*, a spicy sausage-shaped ground meat in a tomato-wine sauce (page 45); capsicums, zucchini, eggplant and tomatoes stuffed with meat and rice (see the Meat and Vegetable sections); lamb stews cooked with vegetables in season (page 56); *stifatho*, a spicy beef and onions (page 54); *pastitso*, a macaroni and meat pie (page 72); and *kapama* (page 62), a rich braise using lamb, young beef or chicken and usually served with pasta or fried potatoes. Grilled lamb, young beef and pork (*sti skaras*), flavoured with *rigani* (the pungent herb used extensively in Greek cooking) and served with the inevitable lemon, is a deliciously simple combination.

At Tourkolimano, restaurants specialising in seafoods line the road opposite the boat-filled bay. In winter, tables are set indoors. Huge piles of giant old oak wine casks reaching to the ceilings are standard décor in most of them.

In summer, tables and chairs are set up on the waterside promenade opposite. Each restaurant is identified by colourful canvas awnings and umbrellas. Food is prepared in the restaurant and carried across to its patrons. The fish comes from the day's catch, and is usually grilled and served with oil and lemon dressing. You can select your fish from those brought over for your inspection, or by going to the restaurant kitchen. It is weighed, cooked to your requirements and priced on its weight.

Around Omonia Square are many take-away food shops which are also restaurants. They offer spit-roasted lamb, pork and chicken (*sti souvla*) and *souvlakia*. Herbed, spicy lamb from the *gyro*, a giant carrot-shaped kebab grilled before a vertical fire, is sliced off deftly as the outside browns, giving the inner meat a chance to cook. When served as take-away fare, the slices are placed in *pita* (flat bread), topped with salad ingredients and folded over.

THE STREET VENDORS AND KAFENIA

The opportunity to eat and drink is ever present in busy, bustling Athens. From early morning through to early morning one need never look far to find someone able to offer sustenance. The *koulourakia* sellers are there, 24 hours a day it seems, with their baskets piled or sticks strung with crisp, sesame-coated rings of yeast bread. When all is quiet they concentrate their efforts around the *kafenia*, where one can have a freshly brewed cup of Greek coffee prepared to taste — *glykos* (very sweet), *metrios* (moderately sweet) or *sketos* (no sugar). A *koulouraki* or two with coffee is often breakfast for early birds or supper for night owls — and a cheap snack at any time of the day, as impoverished young tourists have found.

At sidewalk stands you can buy *tiropita* (*feta*-filled pastries) hot from portable ovens. Or have freshly roasted chestnuts served up in a paper cone from the charcoal brazier of the chestnut seller; when chestnuts are out of season, young corn on the cob takes their place.

The *passo-tempo* man with his basket or trolley of roasted and salted almonds, walnuts, pistachios, peanuts, pine nuts, chick peas, watermelon seeds and sunflower seeds makes his rounds of the tavernas for those who want a salty nibble with their beer or *ouzo*.

The business methods of the various food outlets are quite fascinating. None minds the other dropping in on his clientele. The *kafenion* owner likes the *koulourakia* seller to call on his customers for he, in turn, may have the right to serve a nearby restaurant's diners with coffee. His boy also does the round of nearby offices at mid-morning and collects orders from the office staff. The coffee is carried on a tray suspended on the end of a rod. A cover fits over the steaming cups, keeping heat in and dust out.

The taverna owner welcomes the *passo-tempo* man — why worry if what he sells stimulates thirst! All this sharing of custom is very friendly and very convenient for all concerned.

THE ZAHAROPLASTIA

This epicurean picture of Athens would not be complete without mention of the *zaharoplastis* and the baker. The literal translation of *zaharoplastis* is 'sugar moulder'.

The *zaharoplastion* can be likened to the French patisserie. All manner of sweet delights are available (see pages 86-94 for recipes): tray upon tray of nut-filled syrup or honey-drenched pastries; cakes such as *karithopita, halvas* and *yaourtopita* share space with cakes, tortes and glazed fruit tarts of French origin; cookies such as honey-dipped *melomacarona*, snowy, melt-in-the-mouth *kourabiethes* and sweet, sesame-coated *koulourakia; rizogalo* (creamed rice) and yoghurt, rich chocolate cream rather like a mousse, and *moustalevria* (a type of pudding made from fresh grape juice) crowd the refrigerator. Ice cream in many flavours is served plain or parfait style with berry fruits. The shelves hold fruit liqueurs and jars of spoon sweets made from every conceivable fruit — these are sought by the Athenian housewife to proffer to guests in the home according to tradition. And you can buy from the same shop the china and glass compotes from which to serve the sweets!

Glacé fruits, trays of them, make a most tempting display. The range of fruits prepared in this way is vast, considering the delicate nature of so many of them. Oranges — whole, sliced or as rolls of peel; rolled peel of lemon and grapefruit; small whole figs, pears, nectarines and apricots preserved so well that neither shape nor colour is lost in the lengthy process involved.

Confectionery sold includes toffeed almonds and pistachios, *pasteli* (a sesame and honey wafer), nougat, *loukoumia* and chocolates.

Feast breads make a superb display at Christmas, New Year, Easter and other important days in the Greek Orthodox Church calendar. The Greeks' skill with yeast dough is to be admired.

At Christmas most *zaharoplastia* make a mountain of *kourabiethes*. One shop in Kiffissia, an outer suburb, claims to use 200 kilograms of butter and more than double that in flour to make its mountain. The display can be seen from 20 December, but by New Year's Eve only mounds of powdered sugar remain.

O FOURNAS — THE BAKER

The importance of the baker to the Athenian has not diminished as one might have thought. Although his wares are the staff of life to the Greek as to most races, he still offers a characteristically Greek service. After the day's bread is baked, his oven is used to cook meals brought in by his customers.

In the villages the baker and his oven were, and in some places still are, the centre of daily life. Because few had adequate cooking facilities, roasts, casseroles and trays of cookies would be taken to him for baking. In some areas of Athens this is still practised, at least as far as roasts are concerned. Although the Athenian has modern cooking facilities, many women take the joint of lamb or young beef, the chicken or festive turkey, prepared with its embellishments, to their local baker. For a small fee the baker cooks it, basting and turning when necessary. At midday the roast is collected and carried home for the main meal of the day.

Because it can be so hot in Athens in summer, the housewife prefers to do this rather than heat up her kitchen. It is also a service used by those who work outside the home. One other advantage is the improved flavour of food cooked in a baker's oven.

Enough of talking about the feeling, the flavour and the food of Greece. Try your hand at preparing some of the dishes — then add to, subtract from or vary the recipes as your mood and skill dictate. That is what the Greek cook does. The recipes that follow are a broad sampling of Greek cooking, and have been selected for their popular appeal. As with most cuisines it is a difficult (if not impossible) task to include every recipe and every version of a recipe in one volume, but this selection will have achieved its purpose if it adds Greek dishes to the menus you are proud to prepare.

PICKLED OCTOPUS *OKTAPODI TOURSI*

Serves: 6-8
Cooking time: 45-60 minutes

1 octopus, about 1 kg (2 lb)
1 garlic clove, crushed
½ cup olive oil
½ cup vinegar
salt and pepper to taste

1 To clean octopus, pull off tentacles, remove intestines and ink sac. Cut out eyes and beak. Remove skin and rinse well.
2 Place head and tentacles in a pan without any liquid. Cover and simmer octopus in its own juices over low heat until it turns deep pink and is tender (about 45-60 minutes).
3 Drain and when cool enough to handle strip off suckers from tentacles if desired.
4 Cut head and tentacles into bite-sized pieces and place in a bowl.
5 Add garlic, olive oil, vinegar, salt if necessary and pepper to taste. Mix well, cover and leave to marinate in refrigerator for 12 hours at least before using. Stir occasionally.
6 To serve, lift out of marinade, pile into a dish, garnish with lemon wedges and parsley.
7 Supply cocktail picks for your guests' convenience.

FRIED SQUID   *KALAMARIA TIGANITA*

Serves: 6
Cooking time: 3 minutes

1 kg (2 lb) young squid
salt
flour
lemon wedges
Garlic Sauce (page 39)

1 To clean squid, remove intestines, head and tentacles and pull out transparent backbone. If this is difficult, slit hood open and clean.
2 Wash hoods in cold water and pull off skin.
3 Slice in 5 mm (¼ inch) rings or strips and sprinkle lightly with salt.
4 Coat squid with flour and shallow fry in hot oil a few pieces at a time, turning to brown evenly. Cooking should take no more than 3 minutes.
5 Drain on absorbent paper and place in a hot dish.
6 Serve piping hot with lemon wedges and a bowl of Garlic Sauce.

Note: Young squid do not have their ink sac developed. If squid are large (about 4-5 per 500 g or 1 lb) prepare as above and soak sliced hoods in milk for several hours to tenderise. Drain and cook as above.

STUFFED GRAPE VINE LEAVES   *DOLMATHAKIA LATHERES*

Yield: 6 dozen
Cooking time: 1¼ hours

500 g (1 lb) preserved vine leaves
or
7 dozen fresh young vine leaves
2 large onions, finely chopped
¾ cup olive oil
1 cup short grain rice
3 tablespoons pine nuts

3 tablespoons chopped parsley
2 teaspoons chopped mint
2 teaspoons chopped dill
3 tablespoons currants
salt and pepper
2 cups water
juice of 1 lemon

1 Rinse preserved or fresh vine leaves and blanch in boiling water for 3 minutes, a few at a time. Remove to a bowl of cold water, then drain.
2 Cut off any stems.
3 Gently fry onion in ½ cup olive oil until transparent.
4 Add rice and pine nuts and stir over heat for 2 minutes.
5 Stir in herbs, currants, seasoning to taste and 1 cup water. Cover tightly and cook over low heat for 15 minutes until water is absorbed.
5 To shape rolls, place a leaf, smooth side down, on work surface and put a heaped teaspoon of stuffing in centre. Fold stem end and sides over stuffing and roll up.
7 Line a heavy-based saucepan with a few vine leaves and pack rolls in close together, seam side down.

8 Sprinkle each layer with remaining oil and the lemon juice.
9 Add remaining cup of water and cover top of rolls with leaves.
10 Invert a plate on top to keep rolls in shape during cooking.
11 Cover saucepan tightly, bring to the boil then simmer gently for 1 hour.
12 Remove from heat and leave for 1-2 hours until liquid is absorbed.
13 Lift rolls out carefully into a dish and chill for several hours before serving.
14 Garnish with lemon slices and serve with a bowl of chilled yoghurt.

Note: *Dolmathakia* freeze well — pack into freezer container, seal and freeze. When required allow 24 hours thawing in refrigerator before serving.

If fresh vine leaves are unavailable, use preserved vine leaves in preference to canned vine leaves; preserved vine leaves are usually available in bulk from Greek food speciality shops.

CHEESE TRIANGLES   *TIROPITAKIA*

Yield: 4 dozen
Cooking time: 15-20 minutes
Oven temperature: 180°C (350°F)

Filling:
1 tablespoon butter
1½ tablespoons flour
½ cup milk
125 g (4 oz) feta cheese
60 g (2 oz) tasty cheese, grated
1 egg, beaten

2 tablespoons chopped parsley
¼ teaspoon ground nutmeg
pepper

Case:
500 g (1 lb) filo pastry
¾ cup melted butter

To make filling: Melt butter, stir in flour and cook gently for 1 minute.
2 Add milk and stir over heat until thickened and bubbling.
3 Leave aside to cool.
4 Finely crumble *feta* into a bowl and add grated cheese.
5 Stir in sauce, egg, parsley, nutmeg and pepper to taste.

To shape triangles: Cut each *filo* pastry sheet into three strips approximately 13 × 30 cm (5 × 12 inches). Stack and cover as directed on page 86.
2 Lay a *filo* strip on work surface, brush lightly with melted butter, fold in half lengthways and brush again with butter.
3 Place a level teaspoon of filling on one end of strip.
4 Fold corner of pastry over filling to folded edge to form a triangle. Continue to fold in triangles to end of strip and place seam side down on lightly greased baking trays.
5 Brush tops with melted butter and cook in a moderate oven for 15-20 minutes until puffed and golden brown. Serve hot.

Variation (Spinach Triangles): Use half quantity of Spinach Pie filling (page 79) in place of cheese filling.

Note: Cheese and Spinach Triangles may be prepared and stored in freezer until required for cooking.

EGGPLANT DIP   *MELITZANOSALATA*

Yield: 2 cups
Cooking time: 30-50 minutes
Oven temperature: 180°C (350°F)

1 large or 2 medium oval eggplant to about 500 g (1 lb)
1 garlic clove
salt
¾ cup soft white breadcrumbs

3 tablespoons lemon juice
½ cup olive oil
1 small onion, grated
2 tablespoons chopped parsley
freshly ground black pepper

1 Place whole, unpeeled eggplant on a baking tray and cook in a moderate oven for 30-50 minutes, depending on size, until soft to the touch.
2 While hot remove skin and chop flesh roughly.
3 Have garlic clove crushed with ½ teaspoon salt in a mortar.
4 Gradually add warm eggplant alternately with crumbs.
5 Add lemon juice and olive oil alternately, working mixture thoroughly with pestle.
6 Mix in onion, parsley, additional salt to taste, and pepper.
7 Place in a bowl and chill well. Mixture thickens when thoroughly chilled.
8 Garnish with black olives and serve with crackers, toast fingers or crusty bread.

To make in blender: Place all ingredients except oil in jar of blender.
2 Whirl on low speed until smooth, increase speed and gradually add olive oil; this makes a smoother purée.

Variation: Peel and chop 1 large, ripe tomato and add to mixture with eggplant.

Note: Eggplant discolours quickly once exposed to air, so mixing quickly with other ingredients is important.

FISH ROE PURÉE   *TARAMOSALATA*

Yield: 2 cups

1 tin tarama (100 g or 3½ oz)
1 egg yolk
4 slices stale white bread
1 small garlic clove, crushed
½ small onion, finely grated or minced
3-4 tablespoons lemon juice
½ cup olive oil

1 Put *tarama* and egg yolk in small bowl of electric mixer or in jar of blender and mix on low speed until creamy.
2 Remove crusts from bread and soak bread in cold water. Squeeze dry and add to *tarama* with garlic and onion.
3 Beat until well blended and add lemon juice and olive oil gradually.
4 Increase speed of mixer or blender and mix until light and fluffy.
5 Transfer to a bowl and chill well.
6 Serve with crusty bread, toast fingers, crackers or crisp vegetables such as celery, cucumber and radish.

SOUPS

SPLIT PEA PURÉE   *FAVA*

Serves: 4
Cooking time: 2 hours

2 cups yellow split peas
4 cups water
1 onion, chopped
1½ teaspoons salt
olive oil
lemon wedges

1 Pick over split peas, discarding any that are discoloured. Wash well and place in a heavy-based saucepan.
2 Cover with cold water and bring to the boil.
3 Skim and add chopped onion.
4 Cover and simmer gently without stirring for 2 hours until very soft.
5 Stir in salt and ladle purée into deep plates. Spoon 1-2 tablespoons olive oil onto each serve and accompany with wedges of lemon for squeezing onto purée.

Note: Crusty bread, side dishes of finely sliced onion, black olives and sliced tomato and cucumber in oil and vinegar dressing may also be served with *fava*.

EGG AND LEMON SOUP

AVGOLEMONO SOUPA

Serves: 6
Cooking Time: 25 minutes

6 cups chicken or fish stock
⅓ cup short grain rice or small soup
**   noodles**
salt to taste
3 eggs, separated
juice of 1 large lemon
white pepper

1 Bring stock to boil and add rice or noodles and salt to taste.
2 Stir until stock returns to a slow boil, cover and simmer gently for 20 minutes or until rice or noodles are tender. Skim during cooking if necessary.
3 In a bowl beat egg whites until stiff, add yolks and beat until light and creamy.
4 Gradually beat in lemon juice.
5 Ladle about a quarter of the boiling soup into the eggs, whisking constantly.
6 Remove soup from heat and gradually add egg mixture, stirring vigorously. Keep stirring for 1 minute after egg mixture is added and adjust seasoning with salt and white pepper. Serve immediately.

Note: This soup does not reheat so must be prepared just before serving. Only the stock can be prepared beforehand. Rice or noodles must be cooked in the stock just before it is required for serving.

LENTIL SOUP   FAKI SOUPA

Serves: 4
Cooking time: 1 hour

2 cups lentils
1 large onion, chopped
2 garlic cloves, crushed
⅓ cup olive oil
2 bay leaves
6 cups water
¼ cup wine vinegar
salt and pepper

1 Pick over lentils and wash well.
2 Place in a large pan and add onion, garlic, olive oil, bay leaves and water.
3 Cover pan and bring to the boil.
4 Reduce heat and simmer gently for 1 hour or until lentils are soft.
5 Stir in vinegar and salt and pepper to taste.

6 Serve in deep plates and accompany with crusty bread and salad or a cooked leafy green vegetable dressed with olive oil and lemon juice.

Variation: Heat olive oil and add onion, garlic, 2 diced carrots and ½ cup sliced celery.
2 Fry gently until onion is transparent.
3 Add lentils, bay leaves and water and proceed as above from step number 4.

FISH SOUP   *KAKAVIA*

Serves: 8
Cooking time: stock, 2 hours; soup, 1 hour

1.5 kg (3 lb) fish trimmings
3 litres (5 pints) water
salt and whole peppercorns
2 large onions, chopped
2 garlic cloves, crushed
2 leeks, white part only (optional)
1 cup chopped carrot
1 cup chopped celery, including leaves
½ cup olive oil
2 cups chopped, peeled tomatoes
2 bay leaves

4 sprigs parsley
1 sprig thyme
750 g (1½ lb) potatoes, peeled and sliced
chopped parsley

Fish (see end of 'Method'):
1.5 kg (3 lb) mixed whole fish
500 g (1 lb) green lobster tails
500 g (1 lb) large green prawns
2 tablespoons lemon juice

1 Obtain from fishmonger fish trimmings such as heads and backbones.
2 Rinse well and place in a large pot.
3 Add water, salt and ½ teaspoon peppercorns and simmer for 2 hours.
4 Strain stock and reserve.
5 Gently fry onion, garlic, chopped leeks, carrots and celery in oil for 10 minutes.
6 Add chopped tomatoes, herbs tied into a bunch and reserved fish stock.
7 Season well with salt and freshly ground pepper.
8 Cover and simmer for 30 minutes.
9 Add potatoes and boil for 5 minutes.
10 Reduce heat, add fish pieces and simmer 3 minutes, then add lobster pieces and prawns and simmer for 7-10 minutes until prawns turn pink and lobster meat is cooked. Do not boil when shellfish are added for they will toughen.
11 Pile fish, shellfish and potatoes in a serving dish, sprinkle with chopped parsley and keep hot.
12 Serve soup in a tureen as a first course with crusty bread, then follow with seafoods and potatoes served with lemon wedges and a cruet of olive oil. Alternatively soup, potatoes and seafoods may be served together in deep plates.

Fish and shellfish preparation: Fish suitable are snapper, mullet, eel, whiting, john dory and bream. Cut into 5 cm (2 inch) slices and sprinkle with lemon juice.
2 Add heads and trimmings to fish stock.
3 Cut rinsed lobster tails into 5 cm (2 inch) pieces with shell on.
4 Shell and de-vein prawns.

BEAN SOUP   *FASSOULATHA*

Serves: 6
Cooking time: 2½-3 hours

**2 cups dried beans (black-eyed, haricot
  or lima)**
8 cups hot water
1 large onion, finely chopped
1 garlic clove, crushed (optional)
2 medium carrots, diced
½ cup chopped celery, including leaves
½ cup olive oil
1 cup chopped, peeled tomatoes
1 tablespoon Tomato Paste (page 101)
½ teaspoon sugar
freshly ground black pepper
salt to taste
1 tablespoon chopped parsley

1 Wash beans well and cover with the hot water. Allow to soak for 2 hours;
  overnight soaking can cause beans to ferment and is not necessary.
2 Gently fry onion, garlic, carrots and celery in oil for 10 minutes.
3 Add tomatoes, Tomato Paste, sugar and pepper to taste.
4 Cover and simmer 10 minutes.
5 Add beans and water in which they were soaked, cover and simmer gently for 2
  hours.
6 Add parsley and salt and cook for further 30 minutes to 1 hour until beans are
  tender.
7 Sprinkle with additional chopped parsley and serve with crusty bread, a side
  salad and chilled white wine for a hearty meal. Also good served cold.

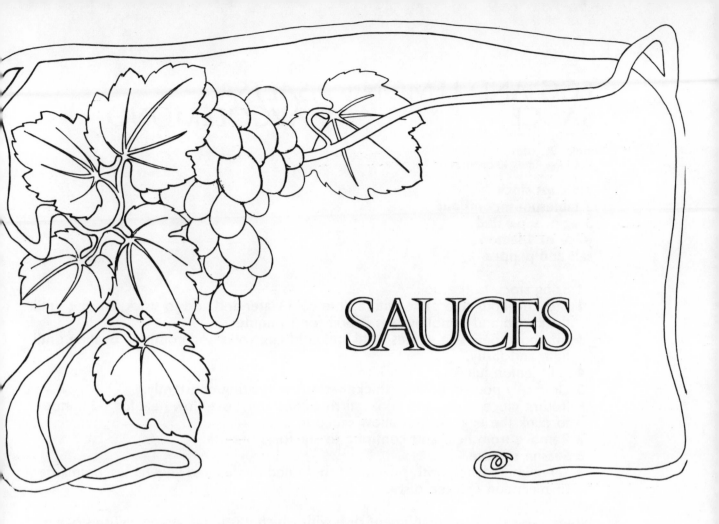

SAUCES

TOMATO SAUCE *SALTSA TOMATA*

Yield: 3 cups
Cooking time: 30 minutes

2 large onions, finely chopped
2 garlic cloves, crushed
3 tablespoons oil or butter
2 cups chopped, peeled tomatoes
2 tablespoons Tomato Paste (page 101)
½ cup dry white wine

1 bay leaf
2 whole cloves
5 cm (2 inch) cinnamon stick (optional)
1 teaspoon sugar
salt and pepper
2 tablespoons chopped parsley

1 Gently fry onion and garlic in oil or butter for 10 minutes or until onion is transparent but not browned.
2 Add remaining ingredients.
3 Cover and simmer gently for 30 minutes.
4 Remove bay leaf, cinnamon stick and cloves. Use as it is or, if a smooth sauce is required, pass through a sieve or purée in blender.
5 Serve on boiled spaghetti or use as directed in recipes.

Note: Make a double quantity and store in a screw-topped jar in refrigerator for convenience. Sauce will keep for 1-2 weeks.

EGG AND LEMON SAUCE

SALTSA AVGOLEMONO

Yield: 2½ cups
Cooking time: 10 minutes

1½ cups stock
1 tablespoon cornflour
3 eggs, separated
juice of 1 lemon
salt and pepper

1 Bring stock to the boil.
2 Mix cornflour to a paste with a little cold water and add to stock, stirring until thickened and bubbling. Let it boil for 1 minute.
3 In a bowl beat egg whites until stiff, add egg yolks and continue beating until light and fluffy.
4 Add lemon juice.
5 Gradually pour in boiling, thickened stock, beating constantly.
6 Return sauce to pan and cook, stirring constantly, over low heat for 1-2 minutes to cook the egg. Do not allow sauce to boil.
7 Remove from heat and continue to stir for 1 minute.
8 Season to taste.
9 Serve immediately with poached fish, boiled or steamed vegetables, *dolmathes* or meat and chicken dishes.

Note: Use stock to compliment dish with which it is to be served — fish stock for poached fish, chicken stock for boiled or steamed vegetables or use cooking liquid from the dish with which it is to be served.

YOGHURT AND CUCUMBER SAUCE

TZATZIKI

Yield: 1¼ cups

1 small cucumber
1 garlic clove, crushed
1 cup yoghurt
2 teaspoons vinegar or lemon juice
1 teaspoon chopped fresh mint or dill
salt to taste

1 Peel cucumber thinly, grate and place in a strainer to drain off excess liquid.
2 Blend grated cucumber and garlic into yoghurt, add vinegar or lemon juice and mint or dill.
3 Season to taste with salt.
4 Serve with fried fish or fried slices of zucchini and eggplant.

Note: This is also served as a salad with cucumber diced instead of grated.

Fish piquant (page 44) and baked fish (page 41).

Braised beef and onions (page 54).

GARLIC SAUCE   *SKORTHALIA*

Yield: 2 cups

6 cloves garlic
salt
1 cup mashed potatoes
2 slices stale white bread
⅓ cup olive oil
1 tablespoon lemon juice
1 tablespoon vinegar
pepper

1 Pound garlic with ½ teaspoon salt in a mortar until smooth.
2 Add mashed potatoes and continue to pound and stir with pestle.
3 Soak bread (crusts removed) in cold water and squeeze dry.
4 Add to potatoes and garlic, pounding and stirring until smooth.
5 Gradually add olive oil, lemon juice and vinegar, stirring vigorously.
6 When smooth and light, add salt and pepper to taste.
7 Chill in a covered bowl before using.
8 Serve with hot or cold seafoods and fried or boiled vegetables.

Variation: Replace bread with ½ cup ground almonds or walnuts, or use 1½ cups ground almonds or walnuts instead of the potatoes and bread.

Blender method: Put all ingredients in jar of blender and blend at moderate speed until ingredients are pulverised.
2 Increase speed for a few seconds until light and smooth. Do not blend too long at high speed for the mixture heats and the oil separates.

MEAT SAUCE   *KIMA*

Yield: 4 cups
Cooking time: 40 minutes

1 large onion, chopped
1 clove garlic, crushed
2 tablespoons oil or butter
500 g (1 lb) ground beef or lamb
1½ cups chopped, peeled tomatoes
2 tablespoons Tomato Paste (page 101)

½ cup red wine
3 whole cloves
1 bay leaf
2 tablespoons chopped parsley
½ teaspoon sugar
salt and pepper

1 Fry onion and garlic gently in oil or butter until onion is transparent.
2 Increase heat and add ground meat.
3 Cook over high heat, stirring frequently, until juices evaporate and meat begins to brown.
4 Lower heat, and add remaining ingredients, seasoning to taste.
5 Cover and simmer gently for 30 minutes.
6 Remove bay leaf and cloves before serving on boiled spaghetti or Rice Pilaf (page 71).

MAYONNAISE *MAYONNEZA*

Yield: 1½ cups

2 egg yolks
½ teaspoon dry mustard (optional)
½ teaspoon sugar
½ teaspoon salt
white pepper
3 tablespoons lemon juice
1 cup olive oil
1 tablespoon boiling water

1 Use a small mixing bowl and a wooden spoon or whisk, or the small bowl on an electric mixer.
2 Remove all traces of egg white from yolks.
3 Stir egg yolks well with mustard (if used), sugar, salt and pepper until light and smooth.
4 Add 2 teaspoons of the lemon juice and about a quarter of the oil, a drop at a time.
5 Blend in remainder of the lemon juice and oil alternately, this time pouring the oil in a thin trickle.
6 When mayonnaise is thick, adjust flavour and seasonings with more lemon juice, salt and pepper if necessary.
7 Last of all beat in boiling water so that mayonnaise will not separate if it is to be stored for some time before use.

Note: Should mayonnaise curdle, begin again by beating an egg yolk in a clean bowl. Gradually add curdled mayonnaise and mixture will begin to emulsify immediately.

OIL AND LEMON DRESSING *LATHOLEMONO*

Yield: 2/3 cup

½ cup olive oil
3 tablespoons lemon juice
2 teaspoons chopped fresh oregano or
  parsley (optional)
½ teaspoon salt
freshly ground black pepper

1 Combine ingredients in a bowl and beat well with a fork until blended.
2 As oil and lemon will separate on standing dressing must be beaten again just before use.
3 Serve with fried fish and on salads. May also be used to brush on fish and shellfish when grilling.

Oil and Vinegar Dressing (Lathoxitho): Substitute vinegar for lemon juice and add ½ teaspoon dry mustard. Prepare as above and serve with raw vegetable salads.

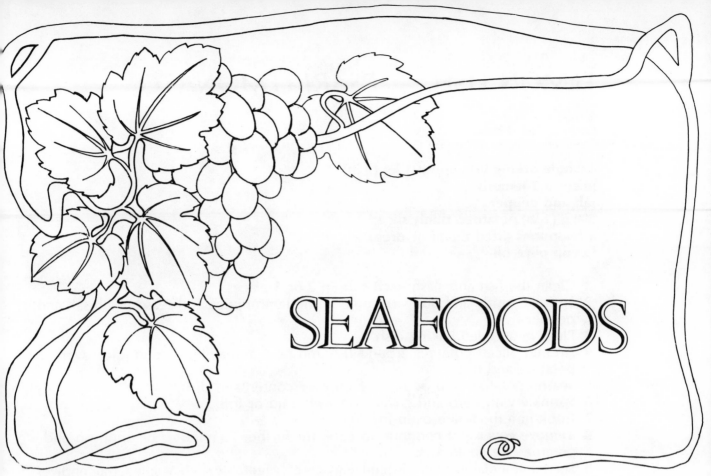

SEAFOODS

BAKED FISH   *PSARI PLAKI*

Serves: 6
Oven temperature: 180°C (350°F)
Cooking time: 1 hour

1.5 kg (3 lb) whole or sliced bream, snapper or mackerel
juice of 1 lemon
salt and pepper
1 large onion, sliced
2 garlic cloves, crushed
½ cup chopped celery, including leaves

½ cup thinly sliced carrot (optional)
½ cup olive oil
2 cups chopped, peeled tomatoes
½ cup dry white wine
½ teaspoon sugar
lemon slices and chopped parsley to garnish

1 Squeeze lemon juice over fish and season with salt and pepper. Cover and leave aside while preparing sauce.
2 Gently fry onion, garlic, celery and carrots in oil until onion is transparent.
3 Add tomatoes, wine, sugar and season to taste.
4 Cover and cook gently for 20 minutes.
5 Spoon some of this sauce into the base of a baking dish.
6 Add fish and top with remaining sauce. If fish slices are used, these can be layered in a casserole dish with the sauce.
7 Cover and cook in a moderate oven for 1 hour. Remove cover after 40 minutes and continue to cook uncovered, basting fish well with sauce during latter stage of cooking.
8 Garnish with lemon slices and chopped parsley and serve with crusty bread, a tossed green salad and chilled white *retsina* wine.

LEMON FISH   *PSARI LEMONATO*

Serves: 5
Cooking time: 1 hour
Oven temperature: 180°C (350°F)

1 whole baking fish, about 1 kg (2 lb)
juice of 2 lemons
salt and pepper
500 g (1 lb) potatoes, thinly sliced
2 teaspoons dried rigani or oregano
½ cup olive oil

1 Clean the fish and slash each side in 2 or 3 places.
2 Sprinkle inside and out with some of the lemon juice and season with salt and pepper.
3 Place in an oiled baking dish.
4 Arrange sliced potatoes around fish and pour remaining lemon juice over potatoes and fish.
5 Season potatoes and pour olive oil over contents of dish.
6 Sprinkle with herb and cover dish with a lid or foil.
7 Cook in a moderate oven for 40 minutes.
8 Remove cover and continue to cook for further 20 minutes or until fish and potatoes are cooked.
9 Serve immediately with a boiled leafy green vegetable such as spinach or endive.

Variation: Add 2 tablespoons drained capers mixed with a little olive oil during last 10 minutes of cooking.

FRIED SALT COD   *BAKALIAROS TIGANITOS*

Serves: 4
Cooking time: 4-5 minutes

500 g (1 lb) dried salt cod
flour
oil for frying
Garlic Sauce (page 39)

Batter:
1 cup plain flour
½ teaspoon salt
1 egg, separated
¾ cup lukewarm water
1 tablespoon oil

1 Cut cod into 8 cm (3 inch) squares and soak in cold water for at least 12 hours, changing water several times.
2 Rinse well and put into saucepan with cold water to cover.
3 Bring slowly to the boil then drain.
4 Remove skin and any loose bones.
5 Dry well, coat pieces with flour and dip into batter.
6 Deep fry 3 or 4 pieces at a time in hot oil until golden brown and crisp.
7 Drain on absorbent paper.
8 Serve hot with Garlic Sauce and beetroot salad.

To make Batter: Sift flour and salt into a bowl.
2 Add egg yolk, water and oil and beat until smooth.
3 Let it stand for 10 minutes, then fold in stiffly beaten egg white.
4 Use immediately.

LOBSTER MAYONNAISE

ASTAKOS MAYONNEZA

Serves: 4
Cooking time: 25 minutes

3 litres (5 pints) cold water
1 tablespoon mustard powder
2 tablespoons salt
½ cup white vinegar

2 live spiny lobsters, each about 1 kg (2 lb)
Mayonnaise (page 40)
parsley to garnish

1 Put cold water, mustard, salt and vinegar in a large pot and bring to the boil.
2 Plunge in the live lobsters, head first, and boil rapidly for 1 minute.
3 Reduce heat and simmer slowly for 25 minutes.
4 Remove lobsters to a bowl of very cold water and leave to cool completely.
5 Cut in half lengthways.
6 Remove stomach, gills and the intestine which runs down the centre of the tail. Reserve any coral present. Lift out tail flesh and slice.
7 Return to shell, spoon some Mayonnaise on top and garnish with parsley and lobster coral (if any).
8 Serve remaining Mayonnaise separately.

Variations: Serve hot or cold lobster with Oil and Lemon Dressing (page 40). If serving hot, do not plunge into cold water — just halve, clean and spoon dressing over flesh.

Grilled lobster: To kill lobster quickly plunge knife into head and split lobster in half lengthways.
2 Clean as above and brush shell and flesh with Oil and Lemon Dressing.
3 Grill under moderate heat or over glowing coals (do the shell side first) for 3-5 minutes.
4 Turn, brush again with dressing and grill for 6-8 minutes or until cooked.
5 Sprinkle with chopped parsley and serve.

Note: Live spiny lobsters are in short supply, but frozen lobster can be just as tasty if thawed correctly.
2 Put cooked or uncooked lobster in a sinkful of cold water .to which a good handful of salt has been added.
3 Leave for about 1 hour until thawed — test by gently pulling back the tail. When thawed it will spring back into position.

43

BAKED PRAWNS WITH FETA

GARITHES ME FETA

Serves: 4
Cooking time: 15-20 minutes
Oven temperature: 220°C (425°F)

750 g (1½ lb) large green prawns
1 cup chopped spring onions
½ cup olive oil
2 garlic cloves, crushed
2 cups chopped, peeled tomatoes
½ cup dry white wine

1 tablespoon chopped parsley
½ teaspoon dried rigani or oregano
½ teaspoon sugar
salt and pepper
90 g (3 oz) feta cheese
finely chopped parsley to garnish

1 Shell prawns leaving last segment of shell and tail intact, and de-vein. Rinse, drain and dry with paper towels.
2 Gently fry onion in oil until transparent, add garlic and cook 1 minute.
3 Add tomatoes, wine, herbs, sugar, salt and freshly ground black pepper.
4 Cover and simmer gently for 30 minutes until very thick.
5 Spoon half of this sauce into 4 individual oven dishes and arrange prawns in each dish.
6 Spoon remaining sauce over prawns and coarsely crumble *feta* cheese on top.
7 Cook in hot oven for 15-20 minutes until prawns are pink and *feta* melts a little.
8 Sprinkle with chopped parsley and serve immediately as a first course.

FISH PIQUANT

PSARI SAVORE

Serves: 6

1 kg (2 lb) fish
seasoned flour
oil for frying
3 garlic cloves, finely chopped
1 teaspoon rosemary spikes
¼ cup wine vinegar
¼ cup dry white wine or water

Any fish suitable for frying may be used — whole fish, fish slices or fillets.
1 Coat with seasoned flour and shallow fry in hot oil until golden brown and cooked through.
2 Drain on absorbent paper and place in a single layer in a serving dish. Keep hot.
3 Drain most of the oil from the pan, leaving about 1 tablespoon.
4 Return pan to heat and add garlic, rosemary and 3 teaspoons of the seasoned flour.
5 Stir well and cook until flour is golden.
6 Remove pan from heat and pour in vinegar, swirling pan contents to blend.
7 Return to heat and stir in wine or water.
8 Let sauce bubble gently for 1 minute.
9 Pour over fish and serve immediately.

Note: Trout is exceptionally good prepared this way.

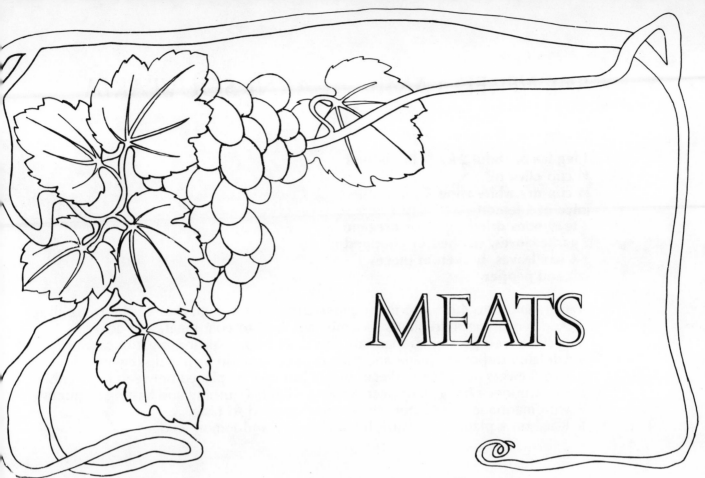

MEATS

SAUSAGES IN TOMATO SAUCE

SOUZOUKAKIA

Serves: 6
Cooking time: 1 hour

500 g (1 lb) finely ground beef
500 g (1 lb) finely ground veal
1 clove garlic, crushed
1 small onion, grated
½ cup dry breadcrumbs
¼ cup sherry or white wine

2 eggs, beaten
1 teaspoon ground cumin
2 teaspoons salt
freshly ground black pepper
oil for frying
2 cups Tomato Sauce (page 35)

1 Mix all ingredients except last two until thoroughly blended, using hands if necessary.
2 Moisten hands with water and shape mixture into sausage-like rolls about 8 cm (3 inches) long.
3 Shallow fry in hot oil until browned on all sides, removing sausages to a heavy-based saucepan as they brown.
4 Drain oil from pan and dissolve cooked-on juices with a little wine or water.
5 Pour over sausages and add prepared Tomato Sauce.
6 Cover and simmer gently for 1 hour.
7 Serve hot with boiled spaghetti, Rice Pilaf (page 71) or fried potatoes and a boiled green vegetable or tossed green salad.

Note: 1 kg (2 lb) ground beef may be used in place of beef and veal.

SKEWERED LAMB   *ARNI SOUVLAKIA*

Serves: 6-8
Cooking time: 15 minutes

1 leg lamb, about 2 kg (4 lb), boned
½ cup olive oil
½ cup dry white wine
juice of 1 lemon
2 teaspoons dried rigani or oregano
2 garlic cloves, crushed or chopped
3-4 bay leaves, broken in pieces
salt and pepper

1 Cut lamb into 4 cm (1½ inch) cubes and place in a glass or earthenware dish.
2 Add remaining ingredients to lamb, mix well to coat meat, and cover.
3 Leave in refrigerator to marinate for 12-24 hours, stirring meat occasionally.
4 Lift lamb out of marinade and thread onto bamboo or metal skewers, allowing two skewers per person. Pieces of bay leaf may be placed between lamb cubes.
5 Cook under a hot grill or over glowing charcoal, turning and basting frequently with marinade, for 15 minutes or until cooked to taste.
6 Place on a platter and garnish with parsley and lemon wedges.

LAMB CHOPS BANDIT STYLE   *ARNI PALIKARI*

Serves: 6
Cooking time: 1¾ hours
Oven temperature: 160°C (325°F)

6 lamb chops or steaks, cut thickly
¼ cup butter or margarine
1 large onion, thinly sliced
3 garlic cloves, finely chopped
4 medium tomatoes

12 thick slices potato
fresh or dried oregano or rigani
salt and pepper
125 g (4 oz) kasseri or Gruyere cheese, sliced
heavy-duty foil

1 Grease a frying pan lightly and fry lamb until browned on each side but not cooked through.
2 Place each chop or steak on a 25 cm (10 inch) square of foil.
3 Drain fat from pan, add butter, onion and garlic and fry gently until onion is soft.
4 Spoon on top of meat, leaving butter in pan.
5 Place 2 slices of potato on each chop and brush with this butter.
6 Top with slices of tomato and sprinkle lightly with oregano or *rigani*.
7 Finish with a slice of cheese on top and fold foil, using double folds to seal each package completely.
8 Place close together in a baking dish (cheese uppermost) and cook in a moderately slow oven for 1½ hours.
9 Serve packages directly onto individual plates. Accompany with a tossed green salad.

Lamb stew with zucchini (page 56).

Vegetable casserole (page 75), snake beans with lemon, stuffed
eggplant (page 81) and braised okra (page 80).

BRAISED HARE WITH ONIONS

LAGHOS STIFATHO

Serves: 6-8
Marinating time: 1-2 days
Cooking time: 3 hours
Oven temperature: 180°C (350°F)

Marinade:
1 onion, chopped
2 garlic cloves, chopped
1 carrot, diced
1 leafy celery top
1 bay leaf
2 sprigs parsley
3 whole cloves
2 cups red wine
freshly ground black pepper

Other ingredients:
1 hare, about 2 kg (4 lb)
½ cup vinegar
2 tablespoons olive oil
2 tablespoons butter
3 tablespoons Tomato Paste (page 101)
1 teaspoon sugar
salt
1 kg (2 lb) small onions

1 Mix marinade ingredients in a bowl, tying herbs in a bunch.
2 Joint hare, put into a bowl and cover with cold water.
3 Add vinegar and leave for 30 minutes.
4 Drain, dry and add to marinade.
5 Cover and leave to marinate for 1-2 days in refrigerator, turning meat occasionally.
6 Lift out of marinade and dry with paper towels.
7 Drain marinade, reserving liquid and vegetables separately — add herbs and cloves to liquid.
8 Brown hare in heated oil and butter.
9 Transfer to a casserole dish.
10 Add marinade vegetables to pan and fry gently for 10 minutes.
11 Add marinade liquid, Tomato Paste, sugar and salt to taste.
12 Bring to the boil and pour over hare.
13 Cover tightly and cook in a moderate oven for 1 hour.
14 Prepare onions (see Braised Beef with Onions, page 54) and add to casserole.
15 Cook for further 1½-2 hours until hare is tender.
16 Remove bunch of herbs, garnish with chopped parsley and serve with mashed potatoes and a green vegetable.

Note: Rabbit may be prepared in the same way.

MEAT PATTIES   *KEFTETHES*

Serves: 6

2 eggs
1 cup soft breadcrumbs
1 large onion, grated
juice of 1 lemon
2 tablespoons chopped parsley
1-2 teaspoons chopped mint (optional)

2 teaspoons salt
freshly ground black pepper
1 kg (2 lb) finely ground beef or lamb
flour for coating
oil for frying

1 Beat eggs lightly in a deep mixing bowl.
2 Stir in breadcrumbs, onion, lemon juice, herbs and seasonings.
3 Leave for 10 minutes.
4 Add meat and blend lightly and thoroughly, mixing with hands if necessary.
5 Cover and refrigerate for 1 hour.
6 With moistened hands shape into balls about the size of a small egg.
7 Roll in flour and flatten to a thick patty.
8 Shallow fry in hot oil until nicely browned (3-4 minutes each side).
9 Lift out and drain on absorbent paper.
10 Place in serving dish as they are cooked and drained, and keep hot until all patties are done.
11 Serve hot with a boiled green vegetable and mashed potatoes or with a tossed salad and fried potatoes.

Variation: Meat Patties with Tomato Sauce *(keftethes me saltsa)*: Prepare 1 quantity Tomato Sauce (page 35), omitting cloves and cinnamon.
2 Spoon over cooked patties and serve as above.

Cocktail Meat Balls (Keftethakia):   Mix as above or substitute 1 tablespoon *ouzo* for lemon juice.
2 Shape into meat balls the size of a small walnut, coat with flour and deep fry in hot oil, a few at a time.
3 Drain and serve hot or cold as an appetiser.
4 Garnish with lemon wedges and parsley.
5 Supply cocktail picks for your guests' convenience.

MEAT BALLS IN SAUCE   *YOUVARLAKIA*

Serves: 6
Cooking time: 1 hour

1 kg (2 lb) finely ground beef or lamb
1 onion, finely chopped
1 egg, beaten
½ cup short grain rice
3 tablespoons chopped parsley

salt and pepper
3 cups light stock
1 tablespoon butter
1 tablespoon cornflour
2 eggs, separated
3 tablespoons lemon juice

1 Mix meat with onion, beaten egg, rice, parsley and salt and pepper to taste.

2 Shape into meat balls the size of a large walnut.
3 Bring stock to the boil and drop in meat balls.
4 Season stock if necessary and add butter.
5 Cover and simmer gently for 1 hour.
6 Strain stock from meat balls into a small saucepan, keeping meat balls hot in the pan.
7 Thicken stock with cornflour mixed with a little cold water and let it simmer for 2 minutes.
8 Beat egg whites until stiff and mix in egg yolks and lemon juice.
9 Add the simmering stock, beating constantly.
10 Pour sauce over meat balls and leave covered, off the heat, for 5 minutes.
11 Sprinkle with a little chopped parsley and serve with mashed potatoes.

Variation: Meat balls may be simmered in Tomato Sauce (page 35) instead of stock. Omit Egg and Lemon Sauce step.

SPIT-ROASTED LAMB   *ARNI STI SOUVLA*

Serves: 40-50
Cooking time: 6-7 hours

1 lamb, about 23 kg (50 lb)
3 lemons
salt and pepper
fresh herbs (thyme, oregano and
  rosemary)
1½ cups olive oil
3-4 garlic cloves, crushed

1 Wipe lamb inside and out with a damp cloth.
2 Rub cavity well with 1 cut lemon, salt and freshly ground black pepper.
3 Put a few sprigs of fresh herbs in the cavity and close with skewers.
4 Rub outer surfaces with cut lemon, salt and pepper.
5 Sit lamb on its stomach and push spit through centre, from between the back legs, along the spine and through the neck.
6 Pull forelegs forwards and tie securely onto the spit with wire.
7 Press back legs along the spit and cross them above it, again securing with wire.
8 Juice 2 lemons and mix with the olive oil, garlic, salt and pepper.
9 Tack a wad of cheesecloth on the end of a rod and tie on a thick faggot of herbs.
10 Leave in the oil and lemon mixture until required for basting.
11 Set a wood fire in a pit or a halved fuel drum and let it burn until flames die down.
12 Add a layer of charcoal and put spitted lamb in position.
13 Turn lamb slowly over fire. Begin with spit well away from fire if possible, then lower closer to fire halfway through cooking.
14 Baste occasionally with oil mixture.
15 Roast for 6-7 hours over the glowing coals, adding more charcoal as needed.

Note: If fire is in a pit, prop sheets of corrugated iron on each side of the fire to deflect the heat onto the lamb.

EGGPLANT MOUSSAKA

MELITZANES MOUSSAKA

Serves: 6-8
Cooking time: 2 hours
Oven temperature: 180°C (350°F)

1 kg (2 lb) eggplant
oil

Meat Sauce:
1 large onion, chopped
2 garlic cloves, crushed
2 tablespoons oil
1 kg (2 lb) ground beef or lamb
1 cup chopped, peeled tomatoes
2 tablespoons Tomato Paste (page 101)
½ cup white wine
2 tablespoons chopped parsley
1 teaspoon sugar
¼ teaspoon cinnamon
salt and pepper

Cream Sauce:
3 tablespoons butter
4 tablespoons flour
2 cups milk
⅛ teaspoon nutmeg or cinnamon
salt and pepper
3 tablespoons grated kefalotiri or parmesan cheese
1 egg, lightly beaten.

1 Cut eggplant into 5 mm (¼ inch) slices with skin on.
2 Sprinkle slices with salt and leave for 1 hour.
3 Dry with paper towels.
4 Oil the base of a baking dish, add a layer of eggplant and brush with oil.
5 Lightly brown under a hot grill, turn, brush again with oil and brown other side. (Alternatively, eggplant may be shallow fried in oil).
6 Stack on a plate when cooked.

To make Meat Sauce: Gently fry onion and garlic in oil for 10 minutes.
2 Add meat and brown over high heat, stirring well.
3 Add remaining meat sauce ingredients, seasoning to taste.
4 Cover and simmer gently for 30 minutes.

To make Cream Sauce: Melt butter in a saucepan, stir in flour and cook gently for 2 minutes.
2 Add milk all at once and bring to the boil, stirring constantly. Let sauce bubble gently for 1 minute.
3 Remove from heat, stir in nutmeg or cinnamon, 1 tablespoon of the cheese, and salt and pepper to taste.
4 Just before spreading on top of Moussaka, stir in the egg.

To finish Moussaka: Grease an oven dish, 33 × 23 × 5 cm (13 × 9 × 2 inches) and place a layer of eggplant slices in the base.
2 Top with half of the meat sauce, add another layer of eggplant, remainder of meat and finish with eggplant.
3 Spread sauce on top and sprinkle with remaining cheese.

4 Bake in a moderate oven for 1 hour.
5 Let stand for 10 minutes before cutting into squares to serve.

Variations: Replace eggplant with an equal quantity of potatoes or zucchini shallow fried in oil, or use a combination of eggplant and potatoes, or zucchini and potatoes.

LITTLE SHOES   *PAPOUTSAKIA*

Serves: 4-8
Cooking time: 1¼ hours
Oven temperature: 180°C (350°F)

4 medium eggplants, each about 250 g (8 oz)
salt
oil for frying
1 large onion, chopped
2 garlic cloves, crushed
2 tablespoons olive oil
500 g (1 lb) ground beef or lamb

1 cup chopped, peeled tomatoes
2 tablespoons chopped parsley
pinch each cinnamon and nutmeg
½ teaspoon sugar
salt and pepper
3 large tomatoes, sliced
grated kefalotiri or parmesan cheese
1 cup water

1 Halve eggplants lengthways.
2 Cut around flesh 5 mm (¼ inch) in from skin, then make 4 deep cuts across and down flesh, taking care not to pierce the skin.
3 Sprinkle cut surfaces with salt and leave for 30-40 minutes.
4 Pat dry and shallow fry in hot oil for 2 minutes on skin side, 5 minutes on flesh side.
5 Cool, scoop out flesh carefully leaving a thin wall.
6 Chop flesh and keep aside.
7 Place eggplant shells in a baking dish.
8 Gently fry onion and garlic in oil for 10 minutes.
9 Increase heat and add meat.
10 Stir well and cook until meat begins to brown.
11 Add tomatoes, parsley, spices, sugar and season with salt and pepper.
12 Cover and simmer gently for 20 minutes.
13 Add reserved eggplant flesh and fill shells.
14 Place 3 or 4 slices of tomato on top of each and sprinkle with cheese.
15 Pour water into base of dish and cook, uncovered, in a moderate oven for 30 minutes.
16 Serve as an entree or as a main course with Country Style Salad (page 85), crusty bread and chilled rosé wine.

Variation: Spread Cream Sauce (see Moussaka, page 52) over filling instead of tomatoes. Also, water in dish may be replaced with 1½ cups Tomato Sauce (page 35).

Note: Medium-sized zucchini may be prepared in the same way.

ROAST LEMON LAMB   *ARNI LEMONATO*

Serves: 6-8
Cooking time: 2½ hours
Oven temperature: 180°C (350°F)

1 × 2 kg (4 lb) leg of lamb
2-3 garlic cloves
juice of 2 lemons
salt and pepper
1 teaspoon dried rigani or oregano
2 tablespoons butter or margarine
1 cup hot water

1 Wipe leg with a damp cloth.
2 Cut small slits over surface of lamb.
3 Cut garlic cloves into slivers and insert in slits.
4 Rub entire surface with lemon juice and season with salt and pepper.
5 Sprinkle with herb and place in a roasting pan.
6 Cook in a moderate oven for 1 hour.
7 Drain off fat and add hot water to pan.
8 Spread butter on lamb and return to oven.
9 Cook for further 1½ hours or until lamb is cooked to taste. Turn during cooking to brown evenly.
10 Allow lamb to rest in a warm place for 15-20 minutes before carving.
11 Skim off excess fat from pan juices, reduce if necessary and serve with the lamb.

Note: 1 kg (2 lb) potatoes, peeled and quartered, may be cooked with the lamb during the last hour. Sprinkle with additional lemon juice and herb if desired.

BRAISED BEEF AND ONIONS   *STIFATHO*

Serves: 6
Oven temperature: 160°C (325°F)
Cooking time: 2-2½ hours

1 kg (2 lb) stewing beef
3 tablespoons butter or oil
1 medium onion, finely chopped
2 garlic cloves, crushed
1 cup tomato purée
½ cup red wine
2 tablespoons wine vinegar

1 bay leaf
8 cm (3 inch) cinnamon stick
4 whole cloves
1 teaspoon sugar
salt and pepper
750 g (1½ lb) small onions
2 tablespoons currants (optional)

1 Cut beef into 5 cm (2 inch) cubes.
2 Brown on all sides in hot butter or oil, placing one layer of meat in pan at a time.
3 Transfer to a casserole dish when browned.

4 Add chopped onion and garlic to pan with more butter if necessary and fry gently until onion is soft.

5 Add tomato purée, wine and wine vinegar and stir to lift pan juices.

6 Pour over meat in casserole.

7 Add bay leaf, spices, sugar and season to taste.

8 Cover and cook in a slow oven for 1 hour.

9 While meat cooks, remove tops and roots from small onions and place in a bowl. Cross-cut root ends to prevent centres popping out during cooking.

10 Cover with boiling water, leave 2 minutes and drain. Skins will slip off easily.

11 Add onions to casserole with currants (if used) and continue to cook for further 1-1½ hours until meat and onions are tender and sauce is thick.

Note: This dish may be cooked slowly on top of the stove.

LIVER PIQUANT   *SIKOTAKIA MARINATA*

Serves: 4

500 g (1 lb) lamb's or calf's liver
salt
flour
oil for frying
2 garlic cloves, finely chopped (optional)
1 teaspoon rosemary spikes or rigani (optional)
¼ cup vinegar
¼ cup dry white wine or water
pepper

1 Remove skin and large tubes from liver, slice thinly and sprinkle with salt.

2 Stand in a cool place for 1 hour.

3 Drain and pat dry.

4 Coat with flour and fry quickly in a little hot oil until browned on each side and just cooked.

5 Place in a serving dish and keep hot.

6 Drain off most of the oil from the pan, leaving about 1 tablespoon.

7 Add garlic and herb (if used) and sprinkle in 2 teaspoons flour.

8 Stir over heat for 2 minutes.

9 Remove from heat and pour in vinegar, taking care since it will sizzle.

10 Return to heat, add wine or water and stir for 1 minute.

11 Pour over liver and let it stand in a warm place for 5 minutes before serving.

12 Serve with mashed potatoes and a green vegetable.

Note: This makes an excellent appetiser.

1 Cut liver slices in 4 cm (1½ inch) squares and proceed as above.

2 Serve hot or cold.

LAMB STEW   *ARNI YAHNI*

Serves: 6
Cooking time: 1½ hours

1 kg (2 lb) boneless lamb shoulder
or
1.5 kg (3 lb) lamb stewing chops
2 tablespoons butter or oil
1 large onion, chopped
2 garlic cloves, crushed
1 carrot, sliced
½ cup sliced celery
1 cup chopped, peeled tomatoes

1 tablespoon Tomato Paste (page 101)
½ cup red or white wine
½ cup stock or water
1 bay leaf
1 tablespoon chopped parsley
½ teaspoon sugar
salt and pepper
prepared vegetable (see end of 'Method')

1 Cut boneless lamb into large cubes; leave chops whole (if used), but trim off excess fat.
2 Brown lamb in butter or oil in a heavy-based saucepan or Dutch oven.
3 Remove to a plate when browned and add onion and garlic to pan.
4 Cook gently until onion is soft, return lamb to pan and add remaining ingredients except main vegetable to be used.
5 Cover and simmer gently for 1 hour.
6 Place prepared vegetable on top of lamb, spooning some of the sauce on top.
7 Cook for further 30 minutes or until lamb and vegetables are tender.
8 Serve with whole boiled or mashed potatoes, unless potatoes are added to the stew, and a tossed green salad.

Vegetable: Prepare 500-750 g (1-1½ lb) of any one of the following vegetables: eggplant; runner beans; potatoes; fresh green peas; zucchini; young broad beans topped and tailed and left whole; 8 cm (3 inch) lengths of blanched celery stalks; fresh or canned okra — if using canned okra add towards end of cooking time.

BRAISED STEAK PIQUANT   *SOFRITO*

Serves: 4-6
Cooking time: 1¼ hours

1 kg (2 lb) young beef steak (topside, round or blade)
seasoned flour
2 tablespoons olive oil
2 tablespoons butter

3 garlic cloves, crushed
¼ cup wine vinegar
1 tablespoon chopped parsley
½ cup water

1 Cut meat into serving-sized portions and coat with seasoned flour.
2 In a frying pan with lid to fit, heat oil and butter and brown meat on both sides.
3 Add garlic, vinegar, parsley and water.
4 Cover and simmer gently for 1 hour or until meat is tender and sauce is thick.
5 Sprinkle with additional chopped parsley and serve with mashed potatoes and a green vegetable.

Globe artichokes (page 76).

Spinach pie (page 79).

STUFFED CABBAGE LEAVES

LAHANO DOLMATHES

Serves: 6
Cooking time: 1½ hours

Stuffing:
1 large onion, finely chopped
1 tablespoon olive oil
1 kg (2 lb) ground beef or lamb
⅓ cup short grain rice
1 tomato, peeled and chopped
2 tablespoons chopped parsley
1 teaspoon chopped dill or mint
⅛ teaspoon ground cinnamon
salt and pepper

Other ingredients:
24 cabbage leaves
2 cups hot stock or water
1 tablespoon butter
salt and pepper
1 tablespoon cornflour
2 eggs, separated
juice of 1 lemon

To make stuffing: Gently fry onion in oil until soft.
2 Mix into meat with remaining stuffing ingredients, seasoning to taste with salt and pepper.
3 Divide into 24 portions.

To make Dolmathes: Blanch cabbage leaves in boiling, salted water for 7 minutes.
2 Drain and cut out thick centre of larger leaves (very large leaves may be cut in half).
3 Place one portion of stuffing on base of leaf, turn up base, fold in sides and wrap firmly into a neat roll.
4 Pack rolls close together, seam side down, in a deep pan lined with a cabbage leaf.
5 Add stock or water, butter, salt and pepper to taste.
6 Invert a heavy plate on top of rolls and cover pan tightly.
7 Simmer gently for 1½ hours.
8 When cooked drain off stock carefully and transfer to a small saucepan.
9 Reduce to 1½ cups over heat and thicken with cornflour mixed to a paste with a little cold water.
10 Let it boil 1 minute.
11 Beat egg whites in a bowl until stiff, add yolks and beat thoroughly.
12 Gradually beat in lemon juice, then boiling stock.
13 Return sauce to pan, place over low heat and stir constantly until egg is cooked — do not boil.
14 Arrange rolls on a heated serving dish and spoon some of the sauce over them.
15 Garnish with chopped dill or parsley and serve remaining sauce separately.
16 Serve with mashed potatoes.

Note: Grape vine leaves may be used instead of cabbage — about 40 will be required since they take less filling.

ROAST SUCKLING PIG

GOUROUNAKI PSITO

Serves: 10-12
Oven temperature: 180°C (350°F)
Cooking time: 4 hours

1 suckling pig, 5-6 kg (10-12 lb)
1½ lemons
salt
olive oil

Stuffing:
1 onion, finely chopped
½ cup finely chopped celery
2 tablespoons butter
250 g (8 oz) ground pork

250 g (8 oz) ground veal
250 g (8 oz) lamb's liver, finely chopped
2 cooking apples, chopped
2 cups short grain rice
3 cups water
1 cup seedless raisins
2 tablespoons chopped parsley
½ teaspoon dried thyme
salt and pepper

1 Rub pig inside and out with one lemon cut in quarters, then rub with salt.
2 Fill with stuffing and close cavity.
3 Place a piece of wood in the mouth.
4 Pull forelegs out and tie, or bend back under body, depending on how well pig fits into oven.
5 Brush all over with oil and place on rack in large roasting pan.
6 Cover snout, ears and tail with foil to prevent burning.
7 Roast in a moderate oven for 4 hours.
8 Baste frequently with lemon half on end of fork dipped in olive oil during first half of cooking, then dipped into pan juices.
9 When cooked remove to platter and replace wood with a red apple.

To make stuffing: Gently fry onion and celery in butter until soft.
2 Stir in ground and chopped meats and cook for 10 minutes.
3 Add remaining ingredients, seasoning to taste.
4 Stir well, cover and cook over gentle heat until liquid is absorbed.

PORK WITH QUINCE

HIRINO ME KITHONIA

Serves: 6
Cooking time: 1¾ hours

1 kg (2 lb) stewing pork, cubed
2 tablespoons butter
2 onions, finely chopped
1 cup red wine
½ cup water
thin strip orange peel

5 cm (2 inch) cinnamon stick
salt and pepper
1 kg (2 lb) quince
1 tablespoon sugar or honey
chopped parsley

1 Brown pork on all sides in butter. Remove to a plate.
2 Add onions to pan and fry gently until soft.
3 Return pork to pan and add wine, water, orange peel and cinnamon.
4 Season to taste with salt and pepper.
5 Cover and simmer for 1 hour.
5 Peel and core quince and slice thickly.
6 Place on top of meat and sprinkle with sugar or add honey.
7 Cover and cook for further 45 minutes or until pork and quince are tender.
8 Garnish with chopped parsley and serve with mashed potatoes.

Note: Veal or beef may be used instead of pork.

STUFFED CAPSICUMS   *PIPERIES YEMISTES*

Serves: 6
Cooking time: 1½ hours
Oven temperature: 160°C (325°F)

12 medium green capsicums
2 medium onions, chopped
2 garlic cloves, crushed
3 tablespoons oil
2 cups chopped, peeled tomatoes
2 tablespoons Tomato Paste (page 101)

¾ cup stock or water
1 teaspoon sugar
salt and pepper
750 g (1½ lb) ground beef or lamb
2 tablespoons chopped parsley
½ cup short grain rice

1 Wash capsicums, cut off tops and reserve.
2 Remove seeds and pith and cook for 3 minutes in boiling, salted water. Lift out and drain.
3 Gently fry onion and garlic in 2 tablespoons of the oil until onion is soft.
4 Add tomatoes, Tomato Paste, stock or water, sugar and season to taste.
5 Cover and simmer for 10 minutes.
6 Heat remaining oil and add meat.
7 Stir well and cook until juices evaporate and meat begins to brown.
8 Add two-thirds of the prepared tomato sauce, bring to the boil and add parsley and rice.
9 Stir well, cover and simmer gently for 10 minutes until liquid is absorbed.
10 Stand capsicums in an oven dish and fill loosely with the meat and rice stuffing.
11 Replace tops on capsicums.
12 Pour remaining tomato sauce into dish and cover with lid or foil.
13 Cook in a moderately slow oven for 45 minutes.
14 Remove cover, baste capsicums with the sauce and cook uncovered for further 10 minutes, adding a little water to sauce if necessary. Serve hot.

Variations: Tomatoes, zucchini and eggplant can be prepared in the same way (do not parboil).
2 To prepare zucchini and eggplant for stuffing, cut off stem ends, scoop out most of flesh, stuff loosely and replace ends, inverting them so that they fit like corks.
3 Lay them side by side in the sauce, turning them over after 30 minutes of cooking.

FRIED BRAINS   *MIALA TIGANITA*

Serves: 4-6
Cooking time: 20 minutes

6 lambs' brains
salt
½ teaspoon whole peppercorns
1 tablespoon lemon juice

1 sprig parsley
flour
butter for frying

1 Soak brains in cold water for 30 minutes. There is no need to skin them.
2 Drain and place in a saucepan, add cold water to cover, salt, peppercorns and lemon juice.
3 Cover and simmer gently for 15 minutes until tender.
4 Drain and dry with paper towels.
5 Cut in 1 cm (½ inch) slices and coat with flour.
6 Fry in hot butter until golden brown.
7 Serve with wedges of lemon.

Variation: After brains are simmered, drain, dry and cut into small cubes or slices.
2 Place in a dish and add Oil and Lemon Dressing (page 40), tossing well to coat brains.
3 Sprinkle with finely chopped parsley and leave to marinate for 2 hours in refrigerator.
4 Serve as an appetiser with toast.

BRAISED MEAT   *KAPAMA*

Serves: 4-6
Cooking time: 1½-2 hours
Oven temperature: 160°C (325°F)

1 kg (2 lb) stewing beef or lamb
2 tablespoons butter or oil
1 large onion, chopped
2 garlic cloves, crushed
1 cup chopped, peeled tomatoes
2 tablespoons Tomato Paste (page 101)

1 small onion studded with 3 cloves
2 bay leaves
8 cm (3 inch) cinnamon stick
1 cup dry red wine
1 teaspoon sugar
salt and pepper

1 Trim meat and cut into 5 cm (2 inch) pieces.
2 Heat butter or oil in a heavy-based saucepan or flameproof casserole and brown meat on all sides, a single layer at a time.
3 Transfer meat to a plate as it browns.
4 Add chopped onion and garlic to pan and fry gently until onion is transparent.
5 Add remaining ingredients.
6 Stir well to lift pan juices and return meat to pan.
7 Cover and simmer on top of stove or cook in a moderately slow oven for 1½-2 hours until meat is tender and sauce thickened.
8 Remove clove-studded onion, bay leaves and cinnamon stick and discard.
9 Serve with boiled spaghetti, grated cheese and a tossed green salad.

Variation: Peel and slice 750 g (1½ lb) potatoes and fry in butter until browned on each side but not cooked through.

2 Add to meat in dish during last 30 minutes of cooking.

3 Serve with a green vegetable or tossed salad.

LAMB FRICASSEE   *ARNI FRICASSE*

Serves 4-6
Cooking time: 1¾-2 hours

1 **large onion, chopped**
2 **tablespoons butter**
1 **kg (2 lb) lean boneless lamb, cubed**
1 **cup hot water**
2 **tablespoons chopped parsley**
1 **teaspoon chopped dill or fennel (optional)**

salt and pepper
prepared vegetable (see end of 'Method')
Egg and Lemon Sauce (page 36)
chopped parsley or dill for garnish

1 In a heavy-based saucepan or Dutch oven gently fry onion in butter until transparent.

2 Increase heat and add cubed lamb. Cook, stirring constantly, until meat juices evaporate. Meat should not brown.

3 Reduce heat and add hot water, herbs and salt and pepper to taste.

4 Cover and simmer gently for 1-1½ hours.

5 Add prepared vegetable and continue to cook until lamb and vegetable are tender.

6 Carefully drain liquid from pan into a measuring jug and make up to 1½ cups with hot water or stock.

7 Keep pan contents hot.

8 Make Egg and Lemon Sauce according to directions.

9 Pour over lamb and vegetable, cover and leave at the side of the stove for 5 minutes.

10 Arrange lamb and vegetable on a serving dish and sprinkle with chopped herb.

11 Serve immediately with crusty bread and a chilled white wine.

Add any one of the following vegetables:

8-12 small globe artichoke hearts (see Globe Artichokes, page 76).
 2 Add to meat after 1 hour and cook for further 30-45 minutes.

500 g (1 lb) celery stalks cut into 8 cm (3 inch) lengths and blanched in boiling, salted water for 5 minutes.
 2 Drain, add to meat after 1 hour and cook for further 45 minutes.
 3 Pork can be used instead of lamb with this vegetable.

4 heads endive, washed well and trimmed of any coarse leaves.
 2 Slit heads in half lengthways and blanch in boiling salted water for 2 minutes.
 3 Drain, add to meat after 1½ hours and cook for further 15 minutes.

4 small firm heads lettuce, washed well and quartered.
 2 Place in colander and scald with boiling water.
 3 Add after 1½ hours and cook for further 15 minutes.

POULTRY

ROAST GOOSE WITH CHESTNUT STUFFING

HINA YEMISTI ME KASTANA

Serves: 8-10
Cooking time: 3½ hours
Oven temperature: 180°C (350°F)

1 goose, about 4 kg (8 lb)
½ lemon
salt and pepper
apples and chestnuts to garnish

Stuffing:
250 g (8 oz) chestnuts
1 small onion, chopped
3 tablespoons butter
4 cooking apples, peeled and diced

1 Remove fat from cavity of goose.
2 Dry well inside and out and sprinkle cavity with salt and pepper.
3 Fill with stuffing (directions follow), secure opening and truss.
4 Rub goose with cut lemon, season well and place on a rack in a roasting pan.
5 Roast in a moderate oven for 3½ hours or until tender.
6 Place goose on a warm platter and leave in a warm place for 20 minutes.
7 Skim fat from pan juices and dilute with a little white wine.
8 Reheat, adjust seasoning and strain into a sauce boat.
9 Garnish goose with apple slices and whole chestnuts fried gently in butter.

64

To prepare stuffing: Shell and peel chestnuts and break in half.
2 Fry onion slowly in butter until soft, add chestnuts and cook for a few minutes longer.
3 Remove from heat and add remaining ingredients.
4 Mix well and fill bird.

LEMON CHICKEN *KOTOPOULO LEMONATO*

Serves: 4
Cooking time: 1½ hours
Oven temperature: 180°C (350°F)

1 chicken, about 1.5 kg (3 lb)
juice of 1 large lemon
salt and pepper

3 tablespoons butter
¼ cup water

1 Wipe chicken and sprinkle some lemon juice, salt and pepper in cavity.
2 Truss and rub skin well with more lemon juice.
3 Season with salt and pepper, put into a buttered casserole dish, cover and refrigerate for several hours or overnight.
4 To cook, spread butter over chicken, add water and cover tightly.
5 Cook in a moderate oven for 1 hour, basting occasionally.
6 Remove lid and cook for further 15 minutes until chicken is golden brown.
7 Serve with juices from dish, rice pilaf and vegetables.

ROAST STUFFED TURKEY *GALLOS YEMISTOS*

Serves: 8-10
Cooking time: 4 hours
Oven temperature: 180°C (350°F)

1 turkey, about 5 kg (10 lb)
2 lemons
salt and pepper
½ cup olive oil or melted butter

Stuffing:
1 onion, finely chopped
½ cup chopped celery
2 tablespoons butter
250 g (8 oz) ground veal

turkey liver, chopped
¾ cup short grain rice
1 cup stock made from remaining giblets
½ cup currants
½ cup pine nuts or chopped walnuts
500 g (1 lb) chestnuts, shelled and peeled
¼ teaspoon ground cinnamon

1 Wipe turkey inside and out with paper towels.
2 Cut 1 lemon into quarters and rub cavities with cut lemon.
3 Sprinkle lightly with salt and pepper.
4 Fill neck and body cavities with stuffing (see end of 'Method', overleaf).

5 Secure openings and truss.
6 Rub skin with cut lemon, then salt and pepper.
7 Place in a roasting dish and brush with olive oil or butter.
8 Cook in a moderate oven for 4 hours, basting every 30 minutes with a mixture of remaining olive oil or butter and juice of remaining lemon.
9 Cover turkey with a piece of foil for first three hours of cooking, remove to brown during last hour.
10 When cooked remove to a warm platter, skim pan juices and strain into a sauceboat.

To make stuffing: Fry onion and celery gently in butter for 10 minutes.
2 Add veal and liver and stir over heat for 5 minutes.
3 Stir in rice and stock, cover pan and cook for 10 minutes.
4 Remove from heat, mix in remaining ingredients and season to taste.

BRAISED CHICKEN *KOTOPOULO KAPAMA*

Serves: 6
Cooking time: 1½ hours

1 chicken, about 2 kg (4 lb)
3 tablespoons butter
1 onion, finely chopped
1 clove garlic, crushed
1½ cups chopped, peeled tomatoes
1 tablespoon Tomato Paste (page 101)

½ cup white wine
1 bay leaf
5 cm (2 inch) cinnamon stick
½ teaspoon sugar
salt and pepper to taste

1 Cut chicken into serving pieces and wipe dry.
2 Melt butter in a heavy saucepan or flameproof casserole and brown chicken on all sides. Remove to a plate when browned.
3 Reduce heat and add onion and garlic.
4 Fry gently until onion is transparent and add remaining ingredients.
5 Return chicken to pan, cover and simmer gently for 45 minutes or until chicken is tender.
6 Remove bay leaf and cinnamon stick and serve *kapama* with boiled macaroni or spaghetti and grated cheese.

Note: Braised Chicken may also be cooked in a moderately slow oven, 160°C (325°F) for 45 minutes to 1 hour.

Variations—Chicken with Okra: Lightly brown 500 g (1 lb) prepared okra (see Braised Okra, page 80) in a little butter.
2 Add to chicken 20 minutes before end of cooking time.
3 Serve with whole boiled or mashed potatoes.

Chicken with Onions: Add 750 g (1½ lb) small whole onions (peeled with root ends cross-cut to prevent centres popping) and 3 whole cloves to sauce with the browned chicken pieces.
2 Cook for 45 minutes to 1 hour.
3 Serve with mashed potatoes and a boiled green vegetable or a tossed salad.

Braised chicken.

Baklava, a perennial favourite among Greek pastries.

CHICKEN PIE   *KOTOPITA*

Serves: 6
Cooking time: 2 hours
Oven temperature: 180°C (350°F)

1 chicken, about 1.5 kg (3 lb)
3 cups water
2 large onions, chopped
1 leafy celery stalk
1 bay leaf
4 parsley stalks
salt and pepper
3 tablespoons butter
5 tablespoons flour
½ cup milk
2 tablespoons grated kefalotiri or
  parmesan cheese
4 eggs, lightly beaten
ground nutmeg
250 g (8 oz) filo pastry
⅓ cup melted butter

1 Place chicken in a pot with water and onions.
2 Tie celery, bay leaf and parsley stalks together and add.
3 Bring to a slow simmer, skim and add salt and pepper.
4 Cover and simmer gently for 1 hour until chicken is tender.
5 Cool a little in the stock and remove to a plate.
6 Bone chicken and dice flesh, discarding skin.
7 Strain stock, discard herbs and reserve onions.
8 Reduce stock to 2 cups over heat.
9 Melt butter in a saucepan, blend in flour and cook gently for 2 minutes.
10 Add the hot stock, stirring constantly until sauce thickens and bubbles.
11 Add milk, bring again to the boil and simmer for 2 minutes.
12 Stir in chicken, reserved onion, cheese and a good pinch of nutmeg.
13 Adjust seasoning and cool.
14 Stir in eggs.

To assemble pie: Grease a 33 × 23 × 5 cm (13 × 9 × 2 inch) baking dish with butter.
2 Line with half of the *filo* pastry sheets, brushing each with butter.
3 Add filling and spread evenly.
4 Top with remaining pastry sheets, again brushing each with butter including top sheet.
5 Tuck in edges of *filo* around pie and score top 3 sheets into squares with a razor blade.
6 Sprinkle lightly with water to prevent *filo* curling and bake in a moderate oven for 45 minutes.
7 Let pie stand for 10 minutes before serving.

Note: 500 g (1 lb) prepared puff pastry may be used instead of *filo*.
2 Bake in a hot oven, 220°C (425°F) for 15 minutes, then reduce to moderate.

PASTA & RICE

MACARONI OR SPAGHETTI   *MACARONADA*

To cook pasta: For 500 g (1 lb) long macaroni or spaghetti, bring 4 litres (7 pints) water to the boil with 2 tablespoons salt and 1 tablespoon oil.

2 Keep water boiling briskly and put in a handful of pasta at a time. Push into the water slowly as the strands soften and curl around the sides of the pan. Stir well as each lot is added, then boil briskly, stirring occasionally.

3 Cook until just tender — test by biting a piece.

4 Drain well in a colander and return to pan in which it was cooked.

To prepare for serving: Melt 3 tablespoons butter for each 500 g (1 lb) pasta.

2 Heat until a deep golden brown — do not burn.

3 Pour over pasta, add 4 tablespoons grated cheese such as *kefalotiri*, Romano or parmesan and toss well to coat strands.

To serve pasta: Place on a hot dish and serve with Tomato Sauce, Meat Sauce or as an accompaniment to Braised Meat and Chicken (*kapama*) — see Index for recipes.

2 Serve extra grated cheese in a bowl.

Note: The oil does not stop the strands sticking together as is often believed, but putting the pasta into the boiling water in long strands does. The oil minimises frothing thus preventing the starchy water boiling over.

PILAF *PILAFI*

Serves: 6
Cooking time: 25 minutes

3 tablespoons butter or margarine
2 cups long or short grain rice
4 cups hot stock
salt and pepper

1 Melt butter or margarine in a heavy-based saucepan and add rice.
2 Stir over moderate heat for 3-5 minutes to colour lightly.
3 Add hot stock, salt and pepper to taste and stir until it begins to boil.
4 Cover tightly and cook over low heat for 12 minutes.
5 Remove from heat and leave covered for 10 minutes.
6 Fluff up with a fork and serve immediately.

A popular way to present Pilaf is to press it into an oiled mould or individual moulds and invert onto a hot dish. A little sauce from the main dish it is to accompany is usually spooned on top.

Note: Choose a stock to compliment dish with which it is to be served — meat, chicken or fish.

Variation—Tomato Pilaf: Gently fry 1 chopped onion and ½ cup chopped green and red capsicums in butter until soft before adding rice.
2 Add 3½ cups stock, 1 cup chopped tomatoes and 1 tablespoon chopped parsley.
3 Proceed as above from step 4.
4 Serve as an accompaniment to roast chicken or lamb.

SPINACH WITH RICE *SPANAKORIZO*

Serves: 6
Cooking time: 20-25 minutes

1 kg (2 lb) spinach or silver beet
1 cup chopped spring onions
1 leek, chopped (optional)
½ cup olive oil
1½ cups short grain rice

2 tablespoons lemon juice
1 tablespoon chopped parsley or dill
3 cups water
salt and pepper

1 Wash spinach or silver beet very well.
2 Remove stems, drain leaves well and tear into pieces. If using silver beet, chop the better stems finely, parboil for 5 minutes in salted water and drain.
3 In a deep pan gently fry onion and leek (if used) in oil until soft.
4 Stir in rice and cook 5 minutes.
5 Add remaining ingredients and parboiled silver beet stems (if used).
6 Bring to the boil and add spinach or silver beet.
7 Stir well, cover and cook gently for 15 minutes.
8 Remove from heat, leave tightly covered and allow to stand for 5 minutes before serving.
9 Serve hot as an accompaniment to main meals, particularly grilled meats and fish.

Note: This is very good served cold.

MACARONI AND MEAT PIE   *PASTITSO*

Serves: 12 as a first course; 6-8 as a main course.
Cooking time: 1½ hours
Oven temperature: 180°C (350°F)

500 g (1 lb) long macaroni
4 tablespoons butter
¾ cup grated kefalotiri or parmesan
  cheese
¼ teaspoon nutmeg
salt and pepper
3 eggs, lightly beaten

Meat Sauce:
1 large onion, chopped   **½ cup red or white wine**
1 garlic clove, crushed   **½ cup stock**
2 tablespoons butter   **2 tablespoons chopped parsley**
750 g (1½ lb) ground beef   **½ teaspoon sugar**
3 tablespoons Tomato Paste (page 101)   **salt and pepper**

Cream Sauce:
⅓ cup butter
½ cup flour
3 cups milk
¼ teaspoon nutmeg
salt and pepper
1 egg, lightly beaten

1 Cook macaroni in boiling, salted water until just tender.
2 Drain and return to pan.
3 Melt butter until golden brown and pour over macaroni.
4 Add ½ cup of the cheese, the nutmeg, salt and pepper to taste and toss well.
5 Leave until cool, add eggs and toss again. Keep aside.

To make Meat Sauce: Gently fry onion and garlic in butter until onion is soft, increase heat and add ground beef.
2 Stir well and cook until meat begins to brown.
3 Add remaining meat sauce ingredients, cover and simmer over gentle heat for 20 minutes.

To make Cream Sauce: Melt butter in a saucepan, stir in flour and cook gently for 2 minutes.
2 Add milk all at once and bring to the boil, stirring constantly.
3 Boil gently for 1 minute.
4 Add nutmeg, salt and pepper to taste and cool a little before stirring in beaten egg.
5 Add ½ cup of this sauce to the cooked meat sauce.

To assemble Pastitso: Butter a 33 × 23 × 8 cm (13 × 9 × 3 inch) oven dish.

2 Spoon half of the prepared macaroni evenly in the base and top with the meat sauce.

3 Cover with remaining macaroni, levelling top.

4 Pour on cream sauce and spread to completely cover macaroni.

5 Sprinkle remaining cheese on top and cook in a moderate oven for 50 minutes until golden brown.

6 Let it stand for 10 minutes before cutting into squares to serve.

STUFFED TOMATOES

TOMATES YEMISTES

Serves: 6
Cooking time: 45 minutes
Oven temperature: 180°C (350°F)

12 medium tomatoes
sugar
salt and pepper
½ cup olive oil
1 large onion, chopped
¼ cup pine nuts (optional)
1½ cups short grain rice
1½ cups hot water
½ cup currants
2 tablespoons chopped parsley
2 tablespoons chopped mint

1 Slice tops from tomatoes and reserve.
2 Scoop out pulp and sprinkle cavities with a little sugar. Keep aside.
3 Put pulp in a saucepan with salt, pepper and ½ teaspoon sugar and simmer until soft.
4 Press through a sieve and reserve.
5 Gently fry onion in half of the oil until transparent.
6 Add pine nuts (if used) and cook for further 5 minutes.
7 Stir in rice, currants, hot water, parsley, mint and season to taste.
8 Bring to the boil, cover and simmer gently for 10 minutes until liquid is absorbed.
9 Fill tomatoes allowing room for rice to swell.
10 Replace tops and stand in an oven dish.
11 Pour puréed tomato pulp and an equal quantity of water (or white wine) into dish.
12 Spoon remaining oil over tomatoes and cook, uncovered, in a moderate oven for 30 minutes.
13 Serve hot or cold.

Note: This makes a pleasant luncheon dish or an attractive accompaniment to main meals.

VEGETABLES

BRAISED ARTICHOKES

AGINARES ALA POLITA

Serves: 6
Cooking time: 30 minutes

12 globe artichoke hearts
½ cup chopped spring onions
500 g (1 lb) baby carrots, scraped
12 button onions, peeled
12 small new potatoes, scraped
juice of 1 lemon

¾ cup olive oil
water or chicken stock
salt and pepper
fresh dill or parsley, chopped
4 teaspoons cornflour

1 Prepare artichoke hearts (see page 76).
2 Line a wide-based saucepan with spring onions.
3 Arrange carrots on top with whole onions, potatoes and artichoke hearts.
4 Add lemon juice, olive oil and enough water or chicken stock to barely cover.
5 Season to taste with salt and pepper and sprinkle 1 tablespoon of dill or parsley over vegetables.
6 Cover and cook over gentle heat for 30 minutes or until vegetables are tender.
7 Remove large vegetables to a heated platter with a slotted spoon, arranging them attractively. Keep hot.
8 Mix cornflour to a paste with a little cold water and thicken liquid in pan — let it boil gently for 2 minutes.
9 Pour sauce over vegetables and garnish with additional chopped herb.

ARTICHOKES WITH EGG AND LEMON SAUCE   *AGINARES ME AVGOLEMONO*

Serves: 6
Cooking time: 40 minutes

6 globe artichokes
juice of 1 lemon
1 tablespoon olive oil

Egg and Lemon Sauce (page 36)
fresh dill or parsley, chopped for garnish

1 Prepare artichokes (see page 76).
2 Cook in boiling, salted water, with lemon juice and oil added, for 30 minutes or until tender. Test by pulling a leaf — if it comes away easily they are done.
3 Lift out with a slotted spoon and invert to drain.
4 Place in a serving dish and keep hot.
5 Make Egg and Lemon Sauce using chicken stock or half stock and half cooking liquid from artichokes.
6 Pour over artichokes and sprinkle with chopped dill or parsley if desired.
7 Serve as a first course.

Variations: Substitute asparagus, broccoli, Brussels sprouts or celery hearts for globe artichokes.
2 Steam or boil according to vegetable used and make sauce with chicken stock.

VEGETABLE CASSEROLE   *BRIAMI*

Serves: 6
Cooking time: 1½ hours
Oven temperature: 180°C (350°F)

1 kg (2 lb) zucchini
500 g (1 lb) potatoes
2 green capsicums
2 garlic cloves, crushed
2 cups chopped, peeled tomatoes
½ teaspoon sugar
2 onions, sliced

salt and pepper
2 tablespoons chopped parsley
2 teaspoons chopped fresh dill or fennel
½ cup olive oil
chopped parsley, dill or fennel to garnish

1 Cut zucchini and potatoes into 1 cm (½ inch) slices.
2 Remove seeds and white membrane from capsicums and slice.
3 Mix together crushed garlic, tomatoes and sugar.
4 Oil an oven dish and arrange some sliced onion on base.
5 Add a layer of prepared vegetables and top with some tomato mixture.
6 Season with salt and pepper and sprinkle on some of the herbs and olive oil.
7 Repeat until all ingredients are used.
8 Cover and cook in a moderate oven for 1-1½ hours until vegetables are tender, removing cover for last 15 minutes.
9 Garnish with additional chopped herbs and serve immediately as a course on its own or as an accompaniment to roast and grilled meats, fish or meat patties.

Variation: Reduce zucchini to 500 g (1 lb) and add equal quantity of eggplant sliced thickly.

GLOBE ARTICHOKES (PREPARATION)

1 Wash artichokes well and cut off stems close to base.
2 Have ready a bowl of cold water with the juice of 1 lemon and some lemon slices added.
3 If desired stir in 2-3 tablespoons flour — this is a typically Greek practice and is quite effective in preventing discolouration.
4 As each artichoke is prepared to requirements, rub cut surfaces with a lemon slice from the bowl and place in the water until all are done.
5 Cook as soon after preparation as possible.

Whole artichokes: Cut off 2.5 cm (1 inch) from top and trim sharp leaf ends with scissors.
2 Remove tough outer leaves and trim carefully around base just enough to neaten.

Artichoke hearts: Cut off 2.5 cm (1 inch) from top and remove 3 or 4 layers of leaves.
2 Scoop out choke with a spoon and cut in half if desired.

Artichoke bases (fonds): Pull off all leaves.
2 Remove choke and trim base into a neat cup shape.

ARTICHOKE OMELETTE   *AGINARES ME AVGA*

Serves: 2
Cooking time: 30 minutes

6 globe artichoke bases
1 cup water
salt
juice of ½ lemon
2 tablespoons butter

4 eggs
4 tablespoons water
1 teaspoon chopped parsley
salt and pepper

1 Prepare artichoke bases (see above).
2 Bring water to the boil, add salt, lemon juice and artichoke bases.
3 Cover and boil gently for 15-20 minutes until tender.
4 Drain and dry.
5 Melt butter in an omelette pan over moderate heat and lightly brown artichoke bases on each side.
6 Beat eggs lightly with the 4 tablespoons water, parsley, and salt and pepper to taste.
7 Pour over artichoke bases in pan, cover with a lid and cook for 5 minutes or until eggs are set on top.
8 Slip onto a plate, put pan on top and invert to return omelette to pan.
9 Cook for further 2-3 minutes until lightly browned on base.
10 Cut in wedges and serve immediately.

Note: This recipe is particularly suited to artichokes which may not be very fresh or are too mature for use as artichoke hearts.

Honey cookies (page 88).

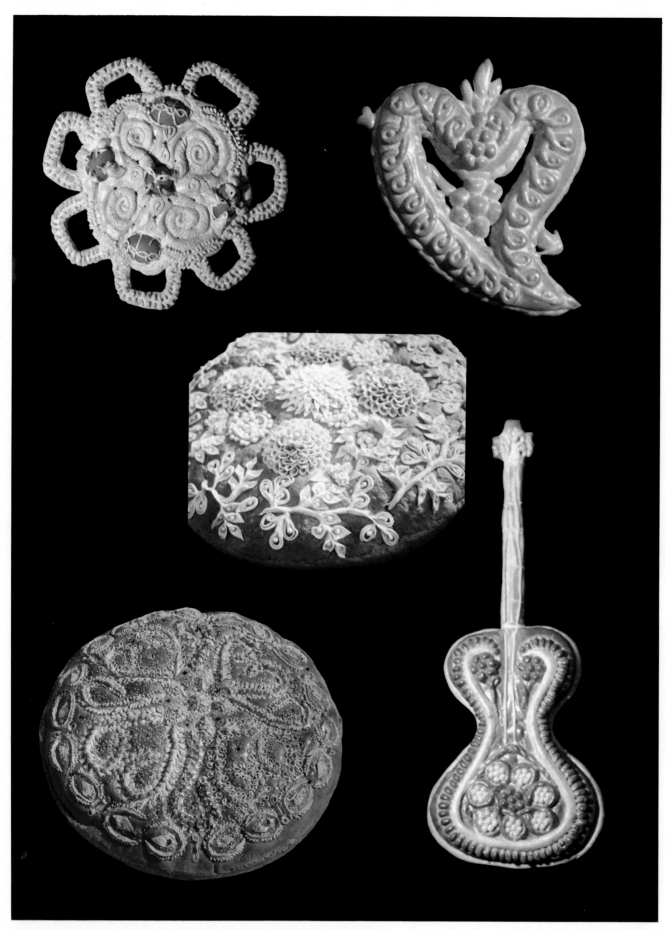

The Greeks bake wedding breads (detail, centre) rather than wedding cakes; the decoration is moulded from a different dough. Christmas bread (bottom left) and Easter breads (page 102) are also imaginatively shaped and decorated.

SPINACH PIE   *SPANAKOPITA*

Serves: 6
Cooking time: 45 minutes
Oven temperature: 190°C (375°F)

1 kg (2 lb) spinach
⅓ cup olive oil
1 cup chopped spring onions
125 g (4 oz) feta cheese, crumbled
1 cup cottage cheese
3 tablespoons grated kefalotiri or parmesan cheese
2 tablespoons chopped parsley
1 teaspoon chopped fresh dill or fennel (optional)
4 eggs, lightly beaten
¼ teaspoon nutmeg
salt and pepper
250 g (8 oz) filo pastry
olive oil for assembling pie

1 Wash spinach well, cut off stems and shake excess water from leaves.
2 Shred coarsely and place in a vegetable steamer or colander over boiling water.
3 Cover and steam for 8 minutes to wilt spinach.
4 Drain off all moisture and place in a bowl to cool.
5 Gently fry spring onions in oil until soft and add oil and onions to spinach.
6 Stir in cheeses, herbs, eggs, nutmeg and season to taste.
7 Lightly oil an oven dish, 35 × 25 cm (14 × 10 inches).
8 Line dish with 5 sheets of *filo* pastry, brushing each sheet with oil.
9 Add spinach filling and spread evenly.
10 Moisten edges of top layer of *filo* with water and place remainder of *filo* on top, brushing each sheet with oil.
11 Trim *filo*, leaving enough to tuck into sides of pie.
12 Brush top with oil and bake in a moderately hot oven for 45 minutes.
13 Remove from oven and let stand for 5 minutes before cutting into squares to serve as a first course. If served as a party snack, score top three layers of *filo* with a razor blade into small squares or diamonds before cooking. Sprinkle top lightly with water after oiling to prevent pastry curling.

Note: Flaky or short crust pastry can replace *filo* — quantity will need to be increased to fit dish used. Silver beet may be used instead of spinach — remove stems and thick white centre section of leaves before weighing. 500-750 g (1-1½ lb) trimmed leaves are sufficient for recipe.

BRAISED OKRA   *BAMYES YAHNI*

Serves: 6
Cooking time: 40-50 minutes

750 g (1½ lb) fresh okra
½ cup vinegar
1 large onion, sliced
2 garlic cloves, crushed
½ cup olive oil

2 cups chopped, peeled tomatoes
1 tablespoon chopped parsley
½ teaspoon sugar
salt and pepper

1 Wash okra and trim stalks but do not remove cone-shaped tops.
2 Place in a bowl, pour over vinegar and leave for 30 minutes — this prevents okra splitting during cooking.
3 Drain, rinse well and dry with paper towels.
4 Gently fry onion and garlic in oil until onion is transparent.
5 Add dried okra and toss gently in pan to brown slightly.
6 Add remaining ingredients, seasoning to taste with salt and freshly ground black pepper.
7 Cover and simmer gently for 30-40 minutes, depending on size of okra, until tender.
8 Sprinkle with additional chopped parsley and serve hot·or cold as a vegetable accompaniment to chicken or grilled lamb.

Variations: Omit okra and vinegar in above recipe and add one of the following vegetables: sliced green beans; sliced zucchini; whole young broad beans, topped and tailed; quartered potatoes; sliced eggplant.

FRIED EGGPLANT   *MELITZANES TIGANITES*

Serves: 4-6
Cooking time: 10 minutes

500 g (1 lb) eggplant
salt
flour or fritter batter (see end of 'Method')
oil for frying
Garlic Sauce (page 39)

1 Wash and dry eggplant.
2 Cut into 5 mm (¼ inch) slices and spread out on trays.
3 Sprinkle with salt and leave for 1 hour.
4 Pat dry with paper towels and coat with flour or fritter batter.
5 Shallow fry in hot oil until golden brown and crisp on each side — 10 minutes in all.
6 Drain on absorbent paper and serve hot with Garlic Sauce.

Fritter batter: Sift 1 cup plain flour and a pinch of salt into a bowl.
2 Add 1 egg yolk, 1 tablespoon oil and ¾ cup lukewarm water.
3 Beat until smooth.
4 Let stand for 10 minutes then fold in stiffly beaten egg white.
5 Use immediately.

Variations—Fried Zucchini: Prepare equal quantity of medium-sized zucchini and proceed as above.

Fried Broad Beans: Wash, top and tail equal quantity of young broad beans, leave whole and parboil in salted water for 5 minutes.
2 Drain, dry, coat with flour and shallow fry.

Fried Cauliflower: Separate 1 head cauliflower into flowerettes and wash well.
2 Parboil in salted water for 6-8 minutes until just tender.
3 Drain and dry.
4 Dip in fritter batter and deep fry in hot oil, a few at a time, until golden brown and crisp.

Note: A mixture of fried vegetables served with Garlic Sauce makes an excellent first course.

STUFFED EGGPLANT   *IMAM BAILDI*

Serves: 4-8
Cooking time: 1¼ hours
Oven temperature: 180°C (350°F)

8 long eggplants, about 1.5 kg (3 lb)
¾ cup olive oil
3 medium onions, halved and sliced
3-4 garlic cloves, cut into slivers
1 tablespoon chopped celery leaves

1 tablespoon chopped parsley
1½ cups chopped, peeled tomatoes
½ teaspoon sugar
salt and pepper

1 Make 4 evenly spaced, deep incisions lengthways in each eggplant and soak in a bowl of salted water for 1 hour to remove bitterness.
2 Drain and dry well, squeezing eggplants gently to remove moisture.
3 Heat ½ cup of the oil in a frying pan and fry eggplants gently on all sides until they begin to soften.
4 Lift out and leave until cool.
5 Add onion and garlic to pan and fry gently until onion is soft.
6 Remove from heat and add remaining ingredients.
7 Stuff some mixture into incisions in eggplants.
8 Place eggplants close together in an oiled oven dish in one layer and pour over remaining oil.
9 Spread any remaining stuffing on top.
10 Cover with lid or foil and cook in a moderate oven for 45 minutes.
11 Serve hot or cold as a first course or as a luncheon dish with crusty bread and chilled white wine.

SALADS

DRIED BEAN SALAD   *FASSOLIA SALATA*

Serves: 6
Cooking time: 2½ hours

1½ **cups dried haricot, lima or black-
   eyed beans**
5 cups hot water
salt
1 small onion, finely chopped
½ cup chopped spring onions

½ cup thinly sliced celery (optional)
2 tablespoons chopped parsley
¼ cup olive oil
wine vinegar to taste
freshly ground black pepper

1 Wash beans well, cover with hot water and leave to soak for 2 hours.
2 Bring to the boil and simmer gently for 2 hours, add salt to taste and cook for
  further 30 minutes or until tender.
3 Drain well and place in a salad bowl.
4 Add remaining ingredients and mix well.
5 Leave until cool, chilling if desired.
6 Garnish with black olives before serving.

Variation—Chick Pea Salad: Substitute an equal quantity of chick peas for dried
  beans.
2 Wash well, add 5 cups cold water and soak overnight — in a cool place if weather is
  warm.
3 Drain, cover with fresh cold water, cook and finish salad as above.

SUMMER SALAD   *SALATA THERINI*

Serves: 6

500 g (1 lb) firm tomatoes, peeled and sliced
2 cucumbers, peeled and sliced
4 spring onions, chopped
1 green capsicum, sliced

1 garlic clove
Oil and Vinegar Dressing (page 40)
salt and pepper
chopped parsley or dried rigani to taste

1 Arrange tomatoes, cucumbers, spring onions and green capsicum in a salad bowl rubbed with cut garlic clove.
2 Beat dressing well and pour over vegetables.
3 Adjust seasoning with salt and freshly ground black pepper and garnish with a sprinkling of parsley or *rigani*.
4 Leave for 10 minutes, toss gently and serve.

Note: Cubes of *feta* cheese and ripe olives may be added if desired.

ZUCCHINI SALAD   *KOLOKITHAKIA SALATA*

Serves: 6-8
Cooking time: 8-10 minutes.

1 kg (2 lb) small zucchini
Oil and Lemon Dressing (page 40)
1 onion, sliced thinly (optional)
chopped parsley

1 If zucchini are very small, trim off stems and leave whole; otherwise slice thinly and cook, uncovered, in boiling, salted water for 8-10 minutes until just tender.
2 Drain well and place in a bowl.
3 Separate onion slices (if used) into rings and add to zucchini with a good sprinkling of chopped parsley.
4 Pour over prepared dressing and toss gently.
5 Chill thoroughly and serve with grilled meats, meat patties and fried or grilled fish.

Note: If you grow your own zucchini, cut them with their flower still on the end.
 2 Trim off stem, leave intact and prepare as above. The flower gives a delightful flavour to the zucchini.

Variations—Green Bean Salad: Replace zucchini with runner beans prepared and sliced French style..

Broccoli Salad: Replace zucchini with broccoli.

EGGPLANT SALAD　　*SALATA MELITZANES*

Serves: 4-6
Cooking time: 20-50 minutes

1 kg (2 lb) eggplant
1 garlic clove, crushed
1 onion, finely chopped
1 green capsicum, cut in strips
2 firm tomatoes, peeled and chopped
1 tablespoon chopped parsley
1 teaspoon dried rigani
½ cup olive oil
2 tablespoons wine vinegar
salt and pepper

1 Place eggplant on grid over glowing charcoals for preference, otherwise place on rack under a hot grill.
2 Cook, turning often, until soft and skin is charred to give a smokey flavour (about 20-30 minutes for long variety of eggplant; 40-50 minutes for large oval eggplant).
3 Peel off skin while hot and dice flesh.
4 Put into a bowl with remaining ingredients adding salt to taste and a good grind of black pepper.
5 Toss well and chill. Excellent with grilled or barbecued meats or fried fish.

BEETROOT SALAD　　*PANTZARIA SALATA*

Serves: 6
Cooking time: 20 minutes

6 young beetroot with tops
salt
Garlic Sauce (page 39)

1 Wash beetroot well.
2 Cut off tops not too close to the bulb.
3 Retain sound, tender leaves, washing them well.
4 Cook beetroot in boiling salted water for 20 minutes or until tender; cook leaves separately in salted water until tender.
5 Skin beetroot while hot and slice into a dish.
6 Drain leaves and add to sliced beetroot.
7 Serve hot or cold with Garlic Sauce served separately.

Note:　Instead of Garlic Sauce, an Oil and Vinegar Dressing may be poured over the beetroot and left to marinate for 2 hours before serving. If vegetable is to be served hot, an Oil and Lemon Dressing may be used.

COUNTRY STYLE SALAD

SALATA EXOHICO

Serves: 6-8

1 quantity Oil and Vinegar Dressing (page 40)
½ garlic clove, crushed
1 head lettuce, imperial or Cos
4 tender spinach leaves
8 tender curly endive leaves
3 firm tomatoes, peeled
1 cucumber, scored and sliced
½ cup black olives
125 g (4 oz) feta cheese, diced
chopped parsley, dill or fennel to taste

Optional ingredients:
1 green capsicum, chopped
4 radishes, sliced
½ cup sliced celery
1 white onion, sliced
1 tablespoon capers
6-8 anchovy fillets
½ teaspoon dried rigani

1 Prepare Oil and Vinegar Dressing and add garlic.
2 Beat well and leave aside until required.
3 Wash salad greens well, shake off excess water and place in a salad basket or tea towel.
4 Swing gently to dry, wrap loosely in a dry towel and chill until crisp.
5 Tear into bite-sized pieces or shred coarsely with a stainless steel knife (the Greek way) and place in a large salad bowl.
6 Add remaining ingredients and any from the optional list which appeal.
7 Beat dressing well and pour over the salad at the table.
8 Toss gently and serve immediately.

Note: Any combination of tender salad greens may be used, depending on what is available. Look for variety in colour tones, texture and flavour.

PASTRIES, CAKES & COOKIES

Two ingredients often used in these recipes are *filo* pastry and syrup. To avoid repetition, details for handling *filo* and for making syrup are given here, unless a recipe calls for a variation. *Filo* is also used for savoury dishes elsewhere in this book, and their recipes refer to this section.

FILO PASTRY

This tissue-thin pastry is available fresh or frozen from Greek delicatessens and bakeries. Some Continental delicatessens sell it as Strudel Pastry.

Three tea towels or glass cloths will be required for the handling of *filo* — two dry and one lightly dampened.

Fresh filo:
1 Remove from wrap and open out onto a folded dry cloth — do not separate sheets.
2 Cover with second folded dry cloth, then with lightly dampened one.
3 Remove each sheet as required, re-covering remainder.

Frozen filo:
1 Remove from wrap and roll up in a dry cloth.
2 Cover with a second lightly dampened cloth.
3 Leave for 2 hours to thaw, then carefully open out *filo* and handle as for fresh *filo*.

Note: *Filo* should not be placed directly into contact with dampened cloths since this makes the pastry too moist and the sheets stick together, resulting in waste. If exposed at room temperature without covering for even a short period, *filo* dries out and is difficult or impossible to handle.

SYRUP

2 cups sugar
2 cups water
3 whole cloves (optional)
5 cm (3 inch) cinnamon stick
1 tablespoon lemon juice
thin strip of lemon rind

1 Place ingredients in a heavy-based saucepan and stir over heat until sugar dissolves.
2 Bring to the boil and boil over moderately high heat for 10 minutes unless otherwise specified.
3 Strain and use hot, lukewarm or cold as required in recipe.

NUT ROLLS   *FLOYERES*

Yield: 5 dozen rolls
Cooking time: 15 minutes
Oven temperature: 190°C (375°F)

500 g (1 lb) filo pastry
1 cup melted, unsalted butter
½ quantity Syrup (see above)

Nut Filling:
1 cup coarsely ground walnuts
1 cup coarsely ground almonds
2 tablespoons caster sugar
½ teaspoon ground cinnamon
1 egg, beaten

1 Cut each sheet of filo into 3 strips, each approximately 12 × 30 cm (5 × 12 inches)
2 Stack and cover as directed on page 86.

To shape rolls: Lightly brush butter on a pastry strip, fold in half lengthways and brush again with butter.
2 Put a teaspoon of nut filling on one end, spreading it out.
3 Roll up *filo* strip firmly into a cylinder.
4 Place finished rolls on greased baking trays.
5 Bake in a moderate oven for 15 minutes until golden brown.
6 Place hot rolls in a single layer in a dish and pour over the hot, strained syrup made as directed above.
7 Leave until cool and drain on a wire rack. Nut rolls keep for 3-4 days; do not store in refrigerator.

To make Nut Filling: Mix ingredients together to form a coarse paste.

HONEY COOKIES   *MELOMACARONA*

Yield: 5 dozen
Cooking time: 20-25 minutes
Oven temperature: 180°C (350°F)

1 cup butter
¾ cup caster sugar
¾ cup maize or peanut oil
grated rind of 1 orange
6 cups plain flour
4 teaspoons baking powder
¾ cup orange juice

Nut Filling (optional):
1 tablespoon honey
1-2 teaspoons orange juice
1½ teaspoons ground cinnamon
1½ cups finely chopped walnuts
2 drops almond essence

Honey Syrup:
½ quantity Syrup (page 87)
¼ cup honey

1 Beat butter and sugar with orange rind until creamy.
2 Gradually add oil and continue beating until mixture is very light and fluffy.
3 Stir in flour alternately with orange juice.
4 Knead dough lightly with hands for 1 minute.
5 Take a scant tablespoon of dough and flatten it a little.
6 Place a teaspoon of the nut filling in the centre and fold dough over to enclose filling.
7 Shape into ovals, pinching ends to a point.
8 Decorate tops with tines of a fork or by crimping cookies diagonally across top in four rows with special crimper (see end of 'Method').
9 Place on lightly greased baking trays and bake in a moderate oven for 20-25 minutes until golden brown.
10 Cool on wire racks.
11 Dip into boiling syrup, four at a time, turning cookies once. Leave in syrup 10 seconds in all, longer if well-soaked cookies are preferred.
12 Lift out onto a plate and leave until cool.

Note: If no nut filling is used, sprinkle tops with crushed walnuts or toasted sesame seeds and cinnamon. Only those which are to be served should be dipped; store remainder in an airtight container and dip when required.

To make Nut Filling: Thin honey down with orange juice and blend into remaining ingredients.

To make Honey Syrup: Make syrup according to directions on page 87, adding honey, but omit cloves.
2 Boil 10 minutes and skim.

3 Let syrup boil on a moderate heat while dipping cookies.
4 Add a little water to syrup when it thickens too much during dipping.

Crimper: Icing crimpers will be familiar to many pastrycooks and cake decorators who work with icing. If you don't own a crimper (or have never seen one), have the family handyman cut a piece of tin or aluminium plate about 2.5 × 10 cm (1 × 4 inches). Bend metal in half over a thin rod and cut 6 to 8 evenly spaced saw-like teeth on the narrow edges. Curl the 'teeth' slightly inwards.

CUSTARD PIE   *GALATOBOUREKO*

Serves: 12
Cooking time: 1 hour
Oven temperature: 180°C (350°F)

4 cups milk
¾ cup sugar
¾ cup fine semolina
¼ cup butter
grated rind of ½ lemon
8 cm (3 inch) cinnamon stick
pinch of salt
5 eggs, lightly beaten
1 teaspoon vanilla essence
250 g (8 oz) filo pastry (page 86)
¾ cup melted, unsalted butter
½ quantity Syrup (page 87)

1 Mix milk, sugar, semolina, butter, lemon rind, cinnamon stick and salt in a heavy-based saucepan and heat until thickened, stirring constantly.
2 Let custard bubble gently over low heat for 5 minutes.
3 Take from heat and remove cinnamon stick.
4 Cover with a piece of buttered paper to prevent skin forming.
5 When cool blend in eggs and vanilla.
6 Butter a 33 × 23 × 5 cm (13 × 9 × 2 inch) oven dish.
7 Place half of the *filo* pastry sheets (about 5 sheets) in the dish, brushing each sheet with the melted butter.
8 Pour in custard and top with remaining sheets, again brushing each with butter as it is placed in position.
9 Brush top with remaining butter and score through top three sheets of *filo* in 8 cm (3 inch) squares or diamonds.
10 Trim edges and bake in a moderate oven for 45 minutes until golden brown and custard is set when tested with a knife.
11 Remove from oven and cool thoroughly in the dish.
12 Make Syrup according to directions on page 87, using half quantity of ingredients listed and omitting cloves.
13 Boil for 12 minutes and cool to lukewarm before straining and pouring over the pie.
14 Leave until cool before serving.

HALVA   *HALVAS*

Serves: 6
Cooking time: 20-25 minutes

1 cup sugar
2½ cups water
½ cup butter
1 cup coarse semolina
2 tablespoons pine nuts or raw peanuts
1 teaspoon cinnamon

1 Dissolve sugar in water and bring to the boil.
2 Boil for 5 minutes. Leave aside.
3 Melt butter in a heavy-based saucepan and stir in semolina and nuts.
4 Increase heat to moderately high and stir constantly until semolina is golden brown (about 10-15 minutes).
5 Remove from heat.
6 Reheat syrup to boiling point and pour into semolina, stirring constantly.
7 Return to low heat, add cinnamon and stir until smooth and bubbling.
8 Cook for 2 minutes.
9 Turn off heat, cover pan with a folded tea towel and put lid on.
10 Leave for 15 minutes then spread *halvas* in a 25 cm (10 inch) pie dish.
11 Decorate top with the tines of a fork in criss-cross fashion and sprinkle with cinnamon.
12 Leave until cool.
13 Cut into diamond shapes to serve as a sweet, snack or dessert.

Note: Make a double quantity and pour into an oiled baba mould when cooked. Decorate with almond slivers or walnut halves and slice to serve as a dessert.

SHORTBREAD COOKIES   *KOURABIETHES*

Yield: 3 dozen
Cooking time: 15-20 minutes
Oven temperature: 180°C (350°F)

1 cup unsalted butter
3 tablespoons icing sugar, sifted
1 egg yolk
1 tablespoon brandy
½ cup finely chopped toasted almonds
  (optional)

2½ cups plain flour
1 teaspoon baking powder
whole cloves
2 cups icing sugar

1 Melt butter until bubbles subside and sediment is golden brown — do not burn.
2 Pour oiled butter into mixing bowl, leaving sediment in pan.
3 When butter has solidified add first quantity of icing sugar and beat on electric mixer until light and fluffy.
4 Add egg yolk and brandy and beat well.

5 Remove bowl from mixer and stir in almonds if used.

6 Sift flour and baking powder twice and mix lightly into butter mixture.

7 Break off small pieces the size of a large walnut.

8 Shape into crescents or roll into balls, place on a flat surface and pinch tops twice, making 4 indentations and at the same time flattening them slightly.

9 Insert a clove into the centre of each cooky.

10 Place cookies on ungreased baking trays and cook in a moderate oven for 15-20 minutes until lightly coloured.

11 Leave to cool on tray for 10 minutes.

12 Sift icing sugar over waxed paper and lift warm cookies onto this.

13 Sift more icing sugar on top and sides.

14 When cool place in a container and sift remaining sugar on top of cookies.

15 Seal and store for 2 days before using to improve the flavour.

16 When serving place each in a small paper cup cake container.

Note: The melting and light browning of the butter is not traditional but it does give a delightful flavour to the cookies. Many excellent Greek cooks use this method, but omit this step if you wish.

SESAME COOKIES *KOULOURAKIA*

Yield: 7 dozen
Cooking time: 15-20 minutes
Oven temperature: 190°C (375°F)

1 cup butter
1½ cups caster sugar
1 teaspoon vanilla essence
3 eggs
5 cups plain flour

3 teaspoons baking powder
½ teaspoon ground cinnamon
¼ teaspoon ground cloves
¼ cup milk
½ cup sesame seeds

1 Cream butter and sugar with vanilla essence until light and fluffy.

2 Beat eggs, reserve 1 tablespoon for glazing and add remainder gradually to butter mixture, beating well.

3 Sift dry ingredients twice and stir into creamed mixture to form a soft dough.

4 Knead a little with hands (if dough is sticky chill for 1 hour — do not add more flour).

5 Scatter some sesame seeds lightly on one side of pastry board.

6 Shape pieces of dough into thick pencil shapes and roll onto the sesame seeds to coat lightly or according to taste.

7 Double over rolled dough and twist, or form into rings, figure eights or coils.

8 Place on greased baking trays and glaze with reserved egg beaten with a little milk.

9 Bake in a moderate oven for 15-20 minutes until golden brown.

10 Cool on a wire rack and store in an airtight container.

Variation: Roll dough in granulated sugar instead of sesame seeds. Glaze lightly with milk.

WALNUT CAKE   *KARITHOPITA*

Cooking time: 45 minutes
Oven temperature: 180°C (350°F)

1 cup butter
1 cup caster sugar
1 teaspoon grated orange rind
4 eggs, separated
1 cup flour
1 cup fine semolina
4 teaspoons baking powder
1 teaspoon ground cinnamon
½ cup milk
2 cups coarsely ground walnuts
1 quantity Syrup (page 87)

1 Cream butter and sugar with orange rind until light and fluffy.
2 Add egg yolks, beating well.
3 Sift flour, semolina, baking powder and cinnamon twice.
4 Fold into creamed mixture alternately with milk and add walnuts, mixing gently.
5 Beat egg whites until stiff and fold into batter using a metal spoon to prevent over-mixing.
6 Pour into a greased oven dish, 33 × 23 × 5cm (13 × 9 × 2 inches).
7 Bake in a moderate oven for 45 minutes or until cooked when tested.
8 Make Syrup while cake is baking.
9 Pour strained, boiling hot syrup over hot cake.
10 When cold cut into squares or diamond shapes and lift out onto serving platter with a pallet knife.
11 Whipped cream may be served separately.

ALMOND PEARS   *AMIGTHALOTA*

Yield: 30
Cooking time: 20 minutes
Oven temperature: 160°C (325°F)

3 cups ground almonds
½ cup sifted icing sugar
¼ cup egg whites (about 2 eggs)
½ teaspoon grated lemon rind
2 drops almond essence
whole cloves
additional icing sugar

1 Blend ground almonds with icing sugar measured after sifting.
2 Add lightly beaten egg whites with lemon rind and almond essence.
3 Mix to a firm dough with hands.
4 Clean hands and rub with a little butter to prevent dough sticking while shaping.
5 Break off small pieces of dough the size of a walnut and form into pear shapes.
6 Insert a whole clove into top of each to resemble stem and place upright on a buttered and floured baking tray.
7 Bake in a moderately slow oven for 20 minutes, covering with brown paper if tops begin to brown.
8 Sift 2 cups icing sugar into a bowl and dip hot Almond Pears into it.
9 Place on a wire rack to cool.
10 Sift remaining sugar from bowl into base of a storage container and arrange cooled Almond Pears upright in a single layer.
11 Sift more sugar thickly over tops and sides, seal and store for a day or two before using.

Note: These are excellent served with after-dinner coffee.

YOGHURT CAKE   *YAOURTOPITA*

Cooking time: 50-60 minutes
Oven temperature: 180°C (350°F)

¾ cup butter
1 cup caster sugar
½ teaspoon grated lemon rind
4 eggs, separated
2½ cups plain flour
1 teaspoon baking powder
1 teaspoon bicarbonate of soda
¼ teaspoon salt
¾ cup yoghurt

1 Cream butter and sugar with lemon rind until light.
2 Add egg yolks and beat well.
3 Sift dry ingredients three times and add to batter alternately with yoghurt.
4 Beat egg whites until stiff and fold gently into batter.
5 Pour into a buttered and floured 23 cm (9 inch) deep-sided cake tin or tube pan and cook in a moderate oven for 50-60 minutes or until cooked when tested.
6 Cool on a wire rack and dust with icing sugar before serving.

Variation: Make a syrup of ½ cup each sugar and water, boiled for 10 minutes with a strip of lemon rind and a small stick of cinnamon.
2 Place cooled cake on a plate and spoon hot, strained syrup over cake — do not dust with icing sugar.
3 Serve with whipped cream as a dessert cake.

BAKLAVA   *BAKLAVA*

Yield: 30 pieces
Cooking time: 1 hour
Oven temperature: 160°C (325°F)

500 g (1 lb) filo pastry (page 86)
¾ cup melted, unsalted butter
2 cups finely chopped walnuts
1 cup finely chopped almonds
¼ cup caster sugar
2 teaspoons ground cinnamon
⅛ teaspoon ground cloves
1 quantity Syrup (page 87)
2 tablespoons honey (optional)

1 Butter base and sides of a 33 × 23 × 5 cm (13 × 9 × 2 inch) oven dish and place nine sheets of *filo* separately into dish, brushing each with melted butter.
2 Mix nuts, sugar and spices and spread half of this mixture over *filo*.
3 Top with another two sheets of *filo*, brushing each with butter.
4 Spread remaining nuts on top and finish with remaining *filo*, brushing each sheet as before.
5 Trim edges and brush top with butter.
6 Score through top layers of *filo* with a sharp knife into diamond shapes.
7 Sprinkle lightly with water to prevent top layers curling upwards.
8 Bake on centre shelf in a moderately slow oven for 30 minutes.
9 Move up one shelf and cook for further 30 minutes.
10 Cover with greased brown paper or foil if top colours too quickly.
11 *Filo* must be allowed to cook thoroughly.
12 When *baklava* goes into the oven, make the Syrup as directed (if honey is used, add with the sugar).
13 Let syrup cool.
14 Spoon strained cool Syrup over hot *baklava*.
15 Leave for several hours before cutting into serving portions.

These glacé fruits include pears, apricots, nectarines, rolled orange and grapefruit peel, figs and whole oranges.

Black and green olives (page 98), pickled peppers (page 99), eggplant
pickle (page 101) and mixed pickles.

PRESERVES

MIXED PICKLES

3 tablespoons rock salt
5 cups water
½ small cauliflower or 4 zucchini
1 green and 1 red capsicum
2 celery stalks
2 green tomatoes

TOURSI

2 carrots
garlic cloves
hot chilli peppers, fresh or dried
fresh dill or fennel sprigs
Spiced Vinegar (see page 99)

1 Stir salt into water and bring to the boil.
2 Leave aside until cool.
3 Wash vegetables well.
4 Break cauliflower into small flowerettes or cut zucchini diagonally into 12 mm (½ inch) slices.
5 Remove seeds and pith from capsicums and cut into thick strips.
6 Slice celery into 5 cm (2 inch) lengths.
7 Slice each tomato into 8-12 wedges.
8 Scrape carrots, cut into thick straws and parboil in salted water for 4 minutes.
9 Place prepared vegetables in a large bowl and cover with cooled brine.
10 Leave for 24 hours, rinse in cold water and drain well.
11 Pack into sterilised jars, adding a halved garlic clove, a hot chilli pepper and a sprig of dill or fennel to each jar.
12 Cover with boiling hot Spiced Vinegar.
13 Seal and store for at least 4 weeks before using.

PICKLING OLIVES

This is the home method of preserving olives when dry salting (see page 16) is not convenient.

If green and ripe olives are mixed together, it is necessary to separate them since the ripe olives take less time to treat.

1 Wash olives well and cut 3 slits in each with a very sharp, fine-bladed stainless steel knife, or (better still) use a razor blade so that the flesh is not bruised.
2 Put olives into glass jars or crocks and cover with cold water.
3 Place a small plate on top to keep olives submerged.
4 Pour water off carefully each day and replace with fresh water, without disturbing olives too much — do this for 3 days for ripe olives, 5 days for green.
5 Pour off and measure the last lot of water to ascertain amount of brine required.
6 Measure that quantity of fresh, warm water into a pan and dissolve enough coarse pickling salt in it so that when an egg is immersed, an area about an inch in diameter breaks the surface. Approximate quantities of salt and water are as follows:

100 g salt to 1 litre water

or

4 oz salt to 1 Imperial pint water

or

3¼ oz salt to 1 U.S. pint water

7 Bring brine to the boil then cool thoroughly before pouring over olives.
8 Float ½ cup olive oil on top of each jar or crock and seal.

The olives can remain indefinitely, but black olives should be ready for eating in 6-8 weeks, green olives in 2-3 months. Olives are ready for use when bitterness has gone.

To prepare for the table: Remove enough olives for 1 month's requirements.
2 Drain well and put into a jar.
3 Cover with vinegar, add 1-2 cut cloves of garlic and float 1 tablespoon olive oil on top.
4 Leave for 1 week before using.

FIG PRESERVES *SYKO GLYKO*

50 small green figs
blanched almonds (optional)
3 cups sugar
3 cups water
1 tablespoon lemon juice
thick strip of grapefruit or lemon peel

1 Wash figs and trim stems.
2 Place figs in a large pan and cover with boiling water.
3 Bring to the boil and boil gently, uncovered, for 15 minutes.
4 Drain and rinse with hot water.
5 Return to pan and cover again with boiling water.

6 Repeat boiling and draining process four times in all.
7 Cook until figs are tender after last change of water (about 1 hour's cooking in all).
8 Drain figs, rinse with cold water and spread out on paper towels to dry.
9 Insert a whole or split almond into base of each fig if desired.
10 In a clean pan bring sugar and water to the boil.
11 Add lemon juice and grapefruit or lemon peel and boil for 10 minutes.
12 Add figs and boil over moderate heat for 10 minutes, skimming when necessary.
13 Cover pan and leave overnight.
14 Next day bring pan contents slowly to the boil and boil gently until syrup is thick when tested.
15 Put figs and syrup into sterilised jars, seal and store in a cool place.

Testing syrup: Drip a little syrup onto a cold plate. If drops do not spread, syrup is ready. If you have a sugar thermometer, cook to a temperature of 105°C (220°F).

PICKLED PEPPERS   *PIPERIES TOURSI*

5 cups water
3 tablespoons rock salt
750 g (1½ lb) long Hungarian peppers
2 garlic cloves
2 hot chilli peppers, fresh or dried

Spiced Vinegar:
5 cups white vinegar
1 tablespoon whole allspice (pimento)
4 cloves
½ teaspoon peppercorns
2 bay leaves
½ cup sugar (optional)

1 Stir salt into water and bring to the boil.
2 Leave until cool.
3 Wash peppers and trim stems without removing them completely.
4 Place peppers in a large bowl and cover with cooled brine.
5 Leave for 24 hours.
6 Drain and rinse thoroughly with cold water.
7 Pack into two sterilised jars adding a halved garlic clove and a hot chilli pepper to each.
8 Cover peppers with strained, boiling hot vinegar and seal.
9 Store for at least 3 weeks before using.

To make Spiced Vinegar: Place vinegar, spices and sugar (if used) in a pan, bring to the boil and simmer gently for 5 minutes.
2 Strain and reheat to boiling point when required.

Note: The traditional Greek pickles do not have sugar, but some cooks use it since it improves the flavour.

PRESERVED ORANGE ROLLS

GLYKO PORTOKALI

6 large, thick-skinned oranges
3 cups sugar
3 cups water
1 tablespoon lemon juice

1 Lightly grate entire surface of each orange.
2 Score peel deeply, from stem end to base, into 6 segments and remove peel carefully.
3 Tightly roll up peel, passing a needle and thread through each roll.
4 When 12 rolls are threaded, tie ends together to form a circle of rolls.
5 Put threaded rolls into a pan of cold water, bring to the boil and drain immediately.
6 Repeat boiling and draining process twice more to remove bitterness from peel.
7 Cover with cold water again and let rolls boil gently until tender.
8 Drain and leave until dry.
9 In a clean pan bring sugar and water to the boil.
10 Add lemon juice and boil syrup for 5 minutes.
11 Add circles of orange rolls and boil for 10 minutes, skimming when necessary.
12 Remove from heat, cover and leave overnight.
13 Next day bring pan contents to the boil and cook gently for 20 minutes or until syrup is thick when tested (see Fig Preserves, page 98).
14 Cool a little, remove threads and place rolls and syrup in sterilised jars.
15 Seal and store in a cool place.

Variations—Grapefruit Rolls: Substitute 4 thick-skinned grapefruit for oranges.
2 After grating rind, cut peel into sixths or eighths, depending on size of fruit.
3 Follow instructions for Orange Rolls.

Lemon Peel Preserves: Substitute 6 thick-skinned lemons for oranges.
2 Cut peel into quarters after grating.
3 Cut each quarter in half to give 8 triangles of peel from each lemon.
4 Do not roll but follow cooking procedure as above. If rolls are desired, do not halve segments — boil just long enough to soften peel, then roll up and thread.

ROSE PETAL JAM

TRIANTAFILLO GLYKO

4 cups fragrant rose petals
3 cups sugar
3 cups water
1 tablespoon lemon juice

1 Wash petals gently and snip off white base of each petal with scissors.
2 Layer petals in a bowl, sprinkling 2 tablespoons of the sugar between each layer.
3 Cover and leave overnight.
4 Next day put remaining sugar and the water on to boil.
5 Add lemon juice and boil for 5 minutes.
6 Remove from heat and cool to lukewarm.

7 Stir in rose petals and return to heat.
8 Bring slowly to the boil and cook gently until jam thickens when tested (see Fig Preserves, page 98).
9 Pour into hot, sterilised jars and seal.

TOMATO PASTE *TOMATA SALTSA*

Yield: approximately 1 kg (2 lb)

5 kg (10 lb) tomatoes
2 tablespoons salt

Choose ripe, sound tomatoes. Do not use any with signs of decay.
1 Wash well, core out stem end and slice into a large preserving pan.
2 Cover and heat gently until tomatoes are soft.
3 Rub through a sieve.
4 Return juice to pan and leave on moderately low heat, uncovered, until reduced by half (tomato purée at this stage.)
5 Pour into 2 large dishes (baking dishes will do) and place in the sun; protect with a covering of gauze.
6 Dry in the sun for 2-4 days, stirring paste now and then. Alternatively place dishes in a cool oven, 100°C (200°F) and let purée evaporate; this will take 4-6 hours.
7 When paste is the consistency of that available commercially (a soft paste), stir in salt and place in sterilised jars.
8 Put a layer of oil on top of paste and seal.
9 Store in a cool place, but once paste is in use, store in refrigerator.

EGGPLANT PICKLE *MELITZANES TOURSI*

1 kg (2 lb) small, long eggplant
salted water
4 garlic cloves
2 leafy celery stalks
1 red capsicum

2 tablespoons chopped parsley
Spiced Vinegar (page 99)
sprigs of dill or fennel
hot chilli peppers

1 Eggplant should be about 5 cm (2 inches) long; remove stems and wash well.
2 Cut a deep incision on each side of fruit and plunge into boiling, salted water.
3 Cover pan and turn off heat.
4 Leave for 5 minutes and drain.
5 Cut garlic into slivers.
6 Slice celery stalks and chop leaves coarsely.
7 Clean capsicum and cut into 2 cm (¾ inch) strips.
8 Mix prepared vegetables with parsley and stuff some of the mixture into incisions in eggplant.
9 Pack into sterilised jars, adding a sprig of dill or fennel and a hot chilli pepper to each jar.
10 Make Spiced Vinegar according to directions, but omit sugar.
11 Pour hot, strained vinegar over eggplants, seal and store for 2 weeks before using.

YEAST BREADS

EASTER BREAD   *TSOUREKI*

Cooking time: 30 minutes
Oven temperature: 190°C (375°F)

30 g (1 oz) compressed yeast
         or
1 package active dry yeast
½ cup lukewarm milk
½ cup melted butter
2 eggs, beaten
1 teaspoon grated lemon rind
½ cup caster sugar
3½ cups plain flour
¼ teaspoon salt
1 teaspoon ground allspice
1 egg for glazing
sesame seeds

  1 Crumble or scatter yeast in ¼ cup of the milk and stir until dissolved.
  2 Add remainder of milk, lukewarm melted butter, eggs, lemon rind and sugar.
  3 Sift flour, salt and spice into a warm bowl and make a well in the centre.

4 Pour in yeast mixture and stir to blend in flour gradually.
5 Mix dough with hands until it comes away from sides.
6 Turn onto a floured surface and knead until smooth and elastic — about 10 minutes.
7 Place ball of dough in a clean bowl brushed with melted butter.
8 Turn dough over to coat top with butter and cover bowl with a cloth.
9 Leave to rise in a warm place until doubled in bulk.
10 Punch down dough and turn onto a floured surface.
11 Knead lightly and tear into three equal portions.
12 Roll each into a rope 30 cm (12 inches) long.
13 Press ends together and plait (braid) loosely, press ends together and tuck under loaf.
14 Place on a greased baking tray, cover with a cloth and leave to rise until doubled — about 1-2 hours depending on warmth.
15 Glaze top with well-beaten egg and sprinkle with sesame seeds.
16 Bake in a moderate oven for 30 minutes until golden brown and cooked when tested (tap base — it will sound hollow when cooked).

Variation: Proceed as above but make each rope 50 cm (20 inches) long.
2 Plait and shape into a ring, pressing the two ends together.
3 Place on a greased baking tray and press four red-dyed eggs at intervals into braid.
4 Prove and cook as directed — sesame seeds may be omitted.

HONEY PUFFS   *LOUKOUMATHES*

Yield: approximately 50
Rising time: 1½ hours

30 g (1 oz) compressed yeast
or
1 package active dry yeast
1 cup lukewarm milk
1 tablespoon caster sugar
1 egg, beaten

¼ cup melted butter
2 cups plain flour
½ teaspoon salt
warm honey
ground cinnamon

1 Dissolve yeast in 2 tablespoons of the lukewarm milk.
2 Add remaining milk, sugar, egg and lukewarm melted butter.
3 Sift flour and salt into a warm bowl and gradually stir in mixed liquids.
4 Beat until smooth and continue beating for 1 minute.
5 Cover with a folded cloth and leave in a warm place for 1½ hours until batter doubles in bulk with bubbles on the surface.
6 Stir well then drop teaspoonfuls into deep, hot oil (190°C or 375°F) — do 4 or 5 at a time.
7 Turn puffs to brown evenly and remove with a slotted spoon (each puff takes about a minute to cook.)
8 Drain on absorbent paper and pile on to a plate.
9 Drizzle each layer with warm honey and sprinkle with cinnamon.
10 Serve hot.

NEW YEAR BREAD   *VASILOPITA*

Cooking time: 45 minutes
Oven temperature: 190°C (375°F)

30 g (1 oz) compressed yeast
                    or
1 package active dry yeast
¾ cup lukewarm milk
½ cup melted butter
3 eggs, beaten
1½ teaspoons grated orange rind
¾ cup caster sugar
4½ cups plain flour
¼ teaspoon salt
½ teaspoon ground cinnamon
½ teaspoon ground nutmeg
egg for glazing
blanched almonds

1　Follow mixing, kneading and proving directions in Easter Bread recipe (page 102).
2　When doubled in bulk punch down and turn on to lightly floured surface.
3　Knead lightly and shape into a round loaf.
4　Place on a large greased baking tray or in a greased 25 cm (10 inch) deep cake tin.
5　Cover and let rise in a warm place until doubled — about 1½-2 hours.
6　Glaze with well-beaten egg and arrange blanched almonds in numbers to denote the New Year, pressing in lightly.
7　Bake in a moderate oven for 45 minutes until golden brown and cooked when tested.
8　If bread browns too quickly place a piece of greased brown paper on top.
9　Cool on a wire rack.

Note:　New Year Bread is traditionally cut at midnight on New Year's Eve. After baking a coin is inserted through a slit in the base. The person who finds the coin will have luck in the New Year.

SUNDRIES

COTTAGE CHEESE *MIZITHRA*

Yield: about 600 g (1¼ lb)

2½ litres (4 pints) milk
3 teaspoons salt
2 rennet tablets
1 tablespoon cold water

1 Heat milk to lukewarm and add salt.
2 Crush rennet tablets in cold water and stir till dissolved.
3 Stir gently into milk.
4 Leave in a warm place for 15 minutes (not on stove) until set.
5 Break up the curds and spoon into a cheesecloth or muslin-lined strainer set over a bowl.
6 Pour off whey as it collects in bowl.
7 Cover and leave in refrigerator for 18 hours to strain curds thoroughly.
8 Turn out onto a dish when firm.
9 Cover and store in refrigerator.

Note: Rennet tablets are available as junket tablets.

YOGHURT   *YAOURTI*

Yield: 4 cups

4 cups fresh milk
½ cup full-cream powdered milk
¼ cup yoghurt (for starter)

1 Reserve ¼ cup fresh milk and stir powdered milk into remainder.
2 Heat milk almost to boiling point and pour into a casserole dish.
3 Leave until lukewarm.
4 Mix yoghurt with reserved milk and stir very gently into milk in dish.
5 Cover dish with lid and wrap carefully in a thick cloth.
6 Leave in a warm place for 6 hours or until thickened. Chill for 4 hours before using.

  Keep a quarter cup of this yoghurt in a sealed jar in the refrigerator until required as a starter for next batch.

Note: Hot milk may be placed into 8 individual moulds. Divide yoghurt and milk mixture evenly between each when lukewarm.

Variation—Skimmed Milk Yoghurt: Replace powdered and fresh milk with 2 cups skimmed milk powder and 3 cups water. Use low-fat yoghurt as starter.

CREAMED RICE   *RIZOGALO*

Serves: 6
Cooking time: 35 minutes

1 cup water
½ cup short grain rice
4 cups milk
pinch of salt
2 egg yolks
2 teaspoons cornflour
2-3 tablespoons sugar
½ teaspoon vanilla essence
ground nutmeg or cinnamon

1 Bring water to the boil in a thick-based saucepan.
2 Stir in rice and cook gently, stirring often, until water is absorbed.
3 Add milk and salt and bring to the boil, stirring occasionally.
4 Cook gently, uncovered, for 20 minutes until rice is very soft.
5 Blend egg yolks with cornflour and a little cold milk.
6 Mix in ½ cup of the hot creamed rice then return to pan contents, stirring over gentle heat just long enough to thicken.
7 Add sugar to taste, and vanilla, and pour into a serving dish or individual bowls.
8 Dust with nutmeg or cinnamon and serve warm or chilled.

GRAPE JUICE PUDDING   *MOUSTALEVRIA*

Cooking time: 10 minutes
Serves: 4

2 cups grape juice
¼ cup sugar
¼ cup fine semolina
pinch ground cloves
⅛ teaspoon ground cinnamon
chopped walnuts or toasted sesame
   seeds
additional ground cinnamon

1 Blend grape juice, sugar and semolina and bring to the boil, stirring constantly, until thickened and bubbling.
2 Add ground cloves and cinnamon and let pudding cook gently for 5 minutes.
3 Pour into individual bowls.
4 Sprinkle liberally with chopped walnuts or toasted sesame seeds and dust lightly with ground cinnamon.
5 Chill before serving.

GREEK COFFEE   *KAFES*

Somehow precise measures do not sound right when writing instructions for the Greek way of making coffee, so forgive the departure from standards already set herein.

You will require a *briki* (a long-handled coffee pot, wide at the base and tapering in at the top), or you can use a small saucepan.

To each demitasse cup of cold water measured into the pot, add 1 heaped teaspoon of powdered (*not* instant) coffee and sugar to taste.

For sweet coffee (*glykos*) add the same amount of sugar; for moderately sweet coffee (*metrios*) add a level teaspoon of sugar; or no sugar, if that is your preference (*sketos*).

Stir over heat only until sugar is dissolved and bring to the boil. The coffee forms a creamy froth on top called *kaimak*. As the froth turns in from the sides and the coffee begins to rise in the pot, remove from heat at once and pour a little into each cup to distribute the froth, then fill cups.

This is just one of the numerous ways to make Greek coffee. Another method requires coffee to be brought to the boil, removed from the heat until it settles down, returned and brought to the boil again — three times in all.

WINES

The Minoans found the product of the grape was good business. They were low on natural resources and it seems wine and oil were fair trade for tin from Spain, copper from Cyprus, gold and pearls from Egypt and ivory from North Africa.

When the Minoan Empire ceased to exist the Mycenaeans took over their trade posts. Ionian and other Greek colonists carried boatloads of wine-filled amphorae to Massilia and Rome. It is to these ancient Greeks that the Gauls and Romans owed their introduction to viticulture, for it did not take them long to realise they could produce their own wines. Roman wine buffs, however, preferred Greek wine to their own vintages, so Greece's exports were not greatly affected until Rome eclipsed Greece.

From then on Greece made wine for its own use and for the stream of uninvited guests who came for varying lengths of time.

Only in recent years have Greek vintners been able to build up their wine exports under their own labels, but the world as a whole is ignorant of Greek wines, many people believing that *retsina* is the only type produced — but attend the Athens Wine Festival held at Daphni for one month from the end of August, or the one held in Rhodes from July 15 to August 31, and that belief will be firmly and finally squashed.

The following is a selection of the wines and spirits available outside Greece, with the producers' names in parentheses:

WHITE WINES
Demestica (Achaia Clauss) — Light, dry wine from Achaia.
Mandinia (Cambas) — Light, dry wine from the Peloponnese.
Robola (Calligas) — Very dry, full-bodied wine from Cephalonia.
Santa Laura (Patraiki) — Crisp, dry wine from Achaia.
St Helena (Achaia Clauss) — Very dry, Riesling style wine from Achaia.

RETSINAS
Patraiki — Dry, white resinated wine from Achaia.
Cambas — White resinated wine from Attica and the Peloponnese.
Achaia Clauss — Dry, white resinated wine from Achaia.

RED WINES
Calligas Rosé (Calligas) — Vintage rosé from Cephalonia.
Castel Danielis (Achaia Clauss) — Red wine, Burgundy style, from Achaia.
Demestica (Achaia Clauss) — Light, dry red wine from Achaia.
Monte Nero (Calligas) — Dry red wine, claret style, from Cephalonia.
Nemea (Cambas) — Dry, full-bodied red wine from Nemea.
Roditis (Patraiki and Cambas) — Rosé wine with the natural colour, aroma and flavour of the roditis grape; from the Peloponnese.

Santa Laura (Patraiki)	Vintage red wine of excellent flavour; from Achaia.
Santa Laura (Patraiki)	Vintage rosé wine from Achaia.

DESSERT WINES
Mavrodaphne (Patraiki, Achaia Clauss and Cambas)	Sweet, rich red wine; also served on the rocks as an aperitif, or in a punch.
Muscat (Patraiki)	Very sweet white wine with the natural aroma and flavour of the grape; from Rion.
Grand Commandaria (Haggipavlu)	Excellent vintage port style wine with an interesting history (it is known as the wine of the Crusaders); from Cyprus.

BRANDY
Greece produces a variety of brandies, some of which compare very favourably with those of France.

Achaia Clauss	Liqueur brandy aged 7 years; from Achaia.
Anglias (Haggipavlu)	Fine brandy from Cyprus.
Cambas	Excellent brandy aged 10 years; from Attica and the Peloponnese.
Metaxas	Full-bodied brandy aged 5 or 7 years; from Piraeus.
Sans Rival	Fine brandy aged 5 years; from Piraeus.

SPIRITS
Ouzo: A clear, aniseed-flavoured spirit, *ouzo* is a by-product of winemaking. It is taken straight, with water, or with ice as an aperitif. Readily available brands include Achaia Clauss, Aphrodite (from Lesbos), Cambas and Sans Rival (from Piraeus).
Mastiha: This is a clear liqueur flavoured with gum mastic. The island of Chios has more than 4 million mastic trees which are tapped for their pale, amber-coloured sap. The sap has been used since ancient times as a chewing gum, and the crushed gum mastic is also used to flavour breads, cookies and confections. Of the *mastiha* available outside Greece, Cambas and Sans Rival are sweet liqueurs, and Sans Rival Mastiha Tavernas (Petros Thomopoulos) is a dry aperitif. The latter hails from Piraeus, and is a very pleasant drink whether taken straight, with water, or with ice.

GLOSSARY

bakaliaros   Dry-salted cod — not to be confused with smoked salt cod. Available at Greek food stores.

eggplant   aubergine

feta   A firm white cheese made from goats' milk. It is easily crumbled.

filo   Tissue-thin pastry available at Greek food stores and bakeries.

kasseri   A creamy, firm cheese with a mild flavour. Gruyère is a good substitute.

kefalotiri   A hard, salty cheese. It grates finely and is used with pasta. Parmesan or Romano are good substitutes.

macaroni   Usually sold in short lengths. The type most often used in Greek cooking comes in long strands and is sometimes called tubular spaghetti.

okra   Also known as ladies' fingers.

pine nuts   Kernels from the cones of the Stone or Umbrella Pine (*Pinus pinea*), a native of the Mediterranean region.

rigani   Wild marjoram, *Origanum vulgare,* available from Greek food stores. The pungent rigani favoured in Greek cooking includes the flower tops with some leaves which are then dried, rubbed well, and stored in an airtight container. Oregano is a slightly milder version of the same herb.

spring onions   Widely known as shallots, although the true shallot has a purple tinge on the outer skin.

spoon sweets   Traditional sweet preserves served to guests in the home. Usually presented in individual dishes, eaten with a spoon and accompanied by iced water.

tarama   Roe of the cod or grey mullet. Available from Greek food stores in tins (locally produced) or in bulk (imported from Greece). You may need to try different brands to find one to your taste.

unsalted butter   sweet butter

zucchini   Also known as courgettes.

FURTHER READING

The following books will be of interest to anyone whose enjoyment of food goes beyond the pleasures of the kitchen and the delights of the table.

Brothwell, D. & P. *Food in antiquity.* Thames & Hudson, London, 1969

Hemphill, John & Rosemary. *Herbs and spices.* Paul Hamlyn, Sydney, 1974

Hippocrates. 4 vols. Loeb Classical Library, London, 1923-31

Polunin, Oleg. *Flowers of Europe.* Oxford University Press, 1969

Schefold, Karl. *Myth and legend in early Greek art.* Thames & Hudson, London, 1966

Vaughn, Agnes Carr. *The house of the double axe.* Weidenfeld & Nicolson, London

Vickery, Kenton Frank. 'Food in early Greece'. In *Studies in the social sciences,* vol. 20, no. 3, 1936. Illinois University

Willetts, R.F. *Everyday life in ancient Crete.* Batsford, London, and Putnam & Sons, New York, 1969

INDEX

Page numbers in **bold** type refer to recipes.